STORIES OF
Kindness

STORIES OF
Kindness

How Singapore came together to battle a pandemic

EDITED BY SOLOMON LIM

Text © The Pride
© 2021 Marshall Cavendish International (Asia) Private Limited

Published in 2021 by Marshall Cavendish Editions
An imprint of Marshall Cavendish International

All rights reserved

No part of this publication may be reproduced, stored in a retrieval system or transmitted, in any form or by any means, electronic, mechanical, photocopying, recording or otherwise, without the prior permission of the copyright owner. Requests for permission should be addressed to the Publisher, Marshall Cavendish International (Asia) Private Limited, 1 New Industrial Road, Singapore 536196. Tel: (65) 6213 9300
E-mail: genref@sg.marshallcavendish.com Website: www.marshallcavendish.com/genref

The publisher makes no representation or warranties with respect to the contents of this book, and specifically disclaims any implied warranties or merchantability or fitness for any particular purpose, and shall in no event be liable for any loss of profit or any other commercial damage, including but not limited to special, incidental, consequential, or other damages.

Other Marshall Cavendish Offices:
Marshall Cavendish Corporation, 800 Westchester Ave, Suite N-641, Rye Brook, NY 10573, USA • Marshall Cavendish International (Thailand) Co Ltd, 253 Asoke, 16th Floor, Sukhumvit 21 Road, Klongtoey Nua, Wattana, Bangkok 10110, Thailand • Marshall Cavendish (Malaysia) Sdn Bhd, Times Subang, Lot 46, Subang Hi-Tech Industrial Park, Batu Tiga, 40000 Shah Alam, Selangor Darul Ehsan, Malaysia

Marshall Cavendish is a registered trademark of Times Publishing Limited

National Library Board, Singapore Cataloguing-in-Publication Data

Name(s): Lim, Solomon, editor.
Title: Stories of kindness : how Singapore came together to battle a pandemic / edited by Solomon Lim.
Description: Singapore : Marshall Cavendish Editions, 2021.
Identifier(s): OCN 1247401922 | ISBN 978-981-4974-23-3
Subject(s): LCSH: Kindness—Singapore. | COVID-19 Pandemic, 2020—Social aspects—Singapore.
Classification: DDC 177.7—dc23

Printed in Singapore

Contents

Message by Mr Edwin Tong — 9
Minister for Culture, Community and Youth

Foreword by Mr Koh Poh Tiong — 11
Chairman, Singapore Kindness Movement

Introduction by Dr William Wan — 12
General-Secretary, Singapore Kindness Movement

Battling Covid-19 — 15

My friend, the frontliner — 16

I survived Covid-19, now I want to help others through tough times — 22

I was stuck overseas after I flew home, away from home — 28

My Stay-Home Notice in a five-star hotel showed me a different side to myself — 33

Covid-19: How I survived a 14-day Stay-Home Notice — 41

"No one is really safe until all of us are safe" — 47

I got married during Covid-19 and it was everything I expected... and not — 53

Finding mental wellness — 59

Covid-19 made me relive my years of struggling with depression — 60

Toxic masculinity needs to stop, and it starts with us — 66

Let's flip the script when we talk about suicide — 73

It's okay not to be okay, so let's talk about it — 80

Parenting our children — 85

"Students who are loved at home, come to school to learn. And students who aren't, come to school to be loved." — 86

A couple's kind act helps Primary 6 pupil reach school in time for PSLE exam	92
Do our grades define us? Learning more about ourselves from our O-Level results	95
How do you talk to your child about their grades?	99
OKLETSGO made me pen a letter to my daughters	104
Raising interracial children: Parents share challenges and opportunities	108
The meaning of Christmas: A family that volunteers together gets the greatest gift of all	114

Being a good neighbour — 123

How do we stop fuming over our neighbour's smoking habit?	124
Would you invite a homeless person to stay in your home?	128
What would you do with crying kids while working from home?	134
I discovered the kampung spirit in an online gathering with total strangers	138

Coming together to help others — 143

Childhood cancer survivor works two jobs during Covid-19, volunteers to help the needy	144
Would you like to learn how to cook from this 85-year-old great grandma?	150
Animal lovers come together to rescue hamsters, guinea pigs and chickens	155
Couple grows community of volunteers to sew clear masks for the deaf	162
These special needs dancers set the stage for more inclusivity and diversity	168

Inclusive café prepares meals for low-income families with special needs children	173
He gives old books and young children a second chance at life	178
She sets up online business to help single mums remember how strong they are	186
Appreciating our migrant workers	**193**
A learning journey showed me the harsh realities migrant workers face every day	194
He searches for foreign workers in forgotten dorms	199
"We spend our best years in Singapore… I don't want us to feel scared of Singaporeans"	203
Celebrating the Singapore spirit	**209**
What makes me a Singaporean?	210
For Singaporeans living overseas, is Singapore really home, truly?	216
193 countries in 17 years: Lessons this Singaporean learnt from visiting every country in the world	222
Let's celebrate racial harmony during the Festival of Lights	231
Racism coloured my childhood and I still fight against stereotypes today	236
Can a UNESCO listing keep Singapore's hawker culture alive?	243
Do you want to know who I voted for in GE2020?	249
About Singapore Kindness Movement	**254**
About The Pride	**255**

Message

by Mr Edwin Tong
Minister for Culture, Community and Youth

2020 will always be remembered as the year that the world came to a standstill because of Covid-19. Singapore was not spared either.

Yet, in spite of the acute stress and concerns from facing an uncertain future caused by an unknown virus, many Singaporeans and members of the community stepped forward to assist and uplift one another. They volunteered their time, skills and resources to care for the vulnerable, and offered mutual aid and support to those around them.

By capturing their stories, this book reminds us that times of crisis are also opportunities to forge a sense of unity, resilience and care for others.

The stories of how people from all walks of life responded to the needs of others – from organising aid and distributing food to migrant workers to creating a platform to match volunteers with elderly and vulnerable residents – show us that regardless of our age, backgrounds or nationalities, we can make a tangible difference to the lives of others. They reaffirm the duties and responsibilities we have to each other and to the common good.

Second, the examples in this book emphasise how we each have a part to play in building our community together. Through actions big and small, we can all contribute to fostering a gracious society where everyone feels a sense of belonging and dignity.

Third, this collection illustrates our individual and collective resolve not to let the stresses and challenges of Covid-19 overwhelm us, and that by reaching out to others and supporting them, we can emerge stronger as a community and society.

I hope that the stories of some of the heroes in our midst will serve as an inspiration and catalyst for all of us to take active steps to Be Greater – and Kinder – in our everyday lives.

Foreword

by Mr Koh Poh Tiong
Chairman, Singapore Kindness Movement

2020 is a watershed moment not just for Singapore but for the world.

In the years to come, people will talk about life before and after Covid-19.

At Singapore Kindness Movement, we have always aimed to inspire graciousness through spontaneous acts of kindness and to make life more pleasant for everyone. Our goals are simple: To encourage all Singaporeans to be kind and considerate, to create public awareness of acts of kindness, and to influence and raise the standards of social behaviour and responsibility.

These goals are simple, but they are not always easy.

During times of crisis, we tend to look inward rather than outward. This is human nature, to protect what's our own first. There are opportunities to be greater, but we don't always take them.

But I'm proud to say that while many things have changed in the new normal, some things haven't. People are still kind and stories of goodness and positivity are still being told.

If anything, we have had more reasons to recognise kindness in 2020, as Covid-19 has made Singaporeans relook their priorities as they deal with their new uncertainties.

That is why I'm so pleased to see that people in Singapore – local and foreign alike – have risen to the occasion. This book of stories, compiled over a year of articles from The Pride, SKM's own content platform, show how we have, in times of trouble, opened our doors and our hearts to those who needed help.

These stories are a celebration of the good we can do, and an inspiration for how much greater we can be.

Introduction

by Dr William Wan
General Secretary, Singapore Kindness Movement

"Why call it The Pride?"

That is a question I am often asked about the moniker that we gave to our digital content platform!

Well, blame it on Singa. He is a lion after all, and his family is called "a pride of lions".

Not only that, we are enormously proud of Singa's tireless efforts in fostering kindness and graciousness since the early days of the National Courtesy Campaign, launched in June 1979.

Now, there is a difference between pride and arrogance, and I daresay as inhabitants of our precious little red dot, we have much to be proud (not arrogant!) of.

For instance, we are the only country in the world to go from third-world to first in one generation. No wonder we are often called a "miracle nation".

We are proud of our airline and our airport. We are proud of our CBD skyline, our manicured garden city, and not to mention our Botanic Gardens, a UNESCO World Heritage site.

More recently, our hawker culture was inscribed on the UNESCO Representative List of Intangible Cultural Heritage. Like that, how not to be proud of Singapore?

Add on our first-class civil service, top universities, impeccable healthcare, efficient public transport, modern infrastructure... and the list goes on.

Oh, so many reasons to be filled with pride!

But there is one intangible I am the most proud of – that we are a kind and gracious people.

I do feel proud of being a Singaporean when foreign friends speak highly about our city in the garden, the beautiful clean waters, its unique architecture, and how Singapore is such a safe place to live, work and play.

But my heart swells so much more when I hear them say: "Your people are so kind and gracious. They are considerate, compassionate, and caring. I will never forget your generous hospitality."

This book is about the kindness shown by so many during this exceedingly difficult season in our nation's life. It is filled with heart-warming accounts of people from all walks of life expressing their innate kindness in so many wonderful ways to friends and strangers alike.

I am filled with pride as I read these inspiring stories. I am sure you will be too.

Battling Covid-19

My friend, the frontliner

We celebrate our frontliners with tributes and cheers, but talking to one – a friend, and a father – truly reminds us about their sacrifices to keep us safe.

by Karun S'Baram

I know Soma through his wife, Uma. Our wives have known each other since secondary school and have kept in touch.

During the circuit breaker, our families would keep in touch over Zoom. It was a nice way of catching up over virtual drinks with the kids chiming in. Both husband and wife are doctors, but we hardly saw Soma, who specialises in Otolaryngology (or ENT), since he worked shifts.

Sometimes, Uma would tell us that he is in the other room. That was odd, until I figured out that Soma was part of the frontline team and was keeping away from his family as much as possible.

As Phase 2 kicked in, in June 2020, I texted him and we arranged to meet for coffee. I wanted to know how my friend handled being a frontliner.

We met at a café at Ng Teng Fong General Hospital where he worked. He was in a casual white shirt and grinned when he saw me. It had been months since we met in person. When he got to my table (I had arrived early), I instinctively reached out to shake his hand, then pulled back in dismay, a haze of "wait, it's Covid, he's a frontliner, am I allowed to shake his hand?" thoughts racing through my head.

I think my kind friend saw the indecision on my face and saved me from further embarrassment by acknowledging me with a namaste instead. We talked shop for a bit and then I asked him about his life.

A day in the life of a doctor on the frontline

A typical day for Soma starts around 6am as he and his wife get their three kids ready before walking them to their nearby primary school. Breakfast is usually prepared and eaten at home.

Then it's off to work at 7.15am with his favourite radio station playing during the morning drive. If Soma is rostered for foreign worker dormitory duty (which happens about two to three times a week) he has to leave even earlier, which means missing breakfast with the kids before they head to school. His day would start with a briefing at the hospital at 7am before the team departs for the dorms.

Being in charge of the medical operations at the dorms means that Soma makes medical decisions on the ground for all foreign workers who report sick for the day. Workers with minor ailments are managed at the dormitory itself but those who appear more sick will be sent by ambulance to the hospital for closer monitoring.

On his regular work days in the hospital, Soma catches up with meetings in the mornings, followed by outpatient clinic consultations or surgeries.

Soma is also on 24-hour emergency call duty seven days a month, where he is on standby any time of the day or night. On such days, he stays at home and catches up on life outside the medical world.

Soma with his family (Dr Uma his wife, Avinaash, Dinesh and Ganga Arthi).
Credit: Soma Subramaniam.

Talking about outside the medical world, he is also Assistant Prof Soma when he's at NUS, since he's also a clinical lecturer for medical students and postgraduate residents.

Although his lectures are now conducted over Zoom, he still conducts small group tutorials with his students. Soma told me how interacting with the students keeps him up to date with the latest publications and literature. This is good for him, he said, adding with a laugh that he now knows about TikTok thanks to his students.

I let out a small chuckle at ourselves, two 40-something men slowly recognising that we are now experiencing from our kids what we used to do to our parents. It's TikTok for the kids now. It was a Walkman during my days.

Then we got interrupted. It was a phone call for Soma. He quickly answered. I noticed that he has his family photo as a screensaver on his nondescript non-flashy handphone. "Do you have to go?" No, it's just a colleague who wanted to reschedule the work roster, he replied.

Then I asked: "Were you worried when you got rostered to the dorms?"

He smiled gently and said that he had concerns and fears, but decided to go ahead as it was the right thing to do at the end of the day.

So, for the initial few weeks from late March, he elected to stay out, living at an assigned hotel room, and then later in a separate room at home. This was probably the toughest period for him, said Soma.

The planning sounded simple and logical but when it was time to do it, the loneliness hit him. He got used to it after a while though, he told me. Talking to his family over the phone and hearing their laughter, knowing that they were safe was good enough!

With strict discipline, Soma adhered to the infection control measures, such as donning protective gear, and the other processes like showering and disinfecting protocols after dormitory operations and strict hand hygiene – all these were able to shield him from the disease, despite the close contact with hundreds of infected foreign workers.

He had to do this daily, and eventually he could sit down and have dinner with his family. But it was worth it, said Soma.

Still, he kept physical interaction to the minimum.

Family concerns and challenges

His wife is also a practising doctor in the public sector. This presented unique challenges as both of them are exposed on a daily basis to the virus. Initially, his older boys were shocked that both mummy and daddy were in contact with Covid patients, but with time, they got used to it.

Not so much Soma's own parents though, who still worry for him. Despite reassuring them on the safety processes and that he is part of a professional team of experts, he still gets frequent phone calls from them.

"My mum got some herbal remedies for me to take to 'boost' my immune system. It tasted horrible but no matter how old you are, you always listen to your mother!" he told me with a laugh.

He misses family time with his kids. Before Covid-19, weekends were spent with the children – helping them with schoolwork, playing with them or just watching a movie together. Cycling as a family around his neighbourhood was a ritual that they have given up too, for now. Just last year, the family started baking together, something Soma told me he enjoys very much (and is pretty good at!). They have stopped doing all that for the time being.

There were also challenges at work. Funnily enough, he said, he missed not being able to eat with his colleagues. Catching up with each other over a quick makan was something they always took for

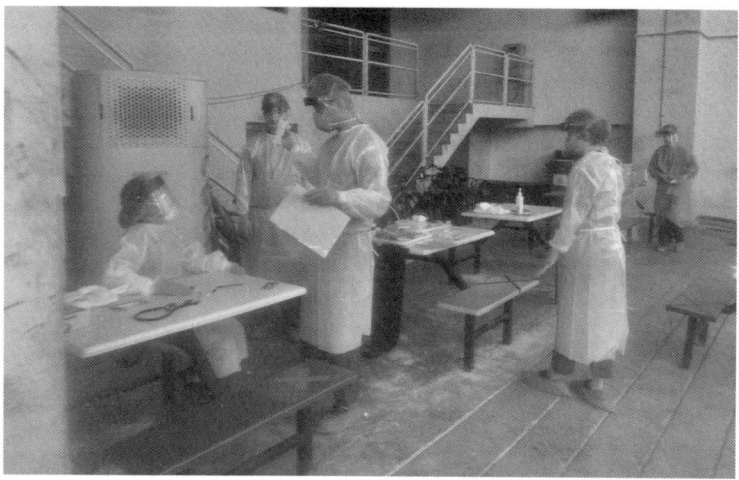

The team at work at one of the foreign worker dormitories. *Credit: Ng Teng Fong General Hospital.*

granted and he hopes to be able to do that again soon. I told him that that day will come sooner rather than later, thanks to him and all our Covid-19 heroes.

But Soma doesn't just have to deal with the daily grind of being in the frontline.

He told me: "There was this recent case of a Covid patient who was critically ill and needed a surgical tracheostomy [surgery done to wean him off the mechanical ventilator]. The surgery itself was particularly challenging, as I had to wear a PAPR [powered air-purifying respirator], also known as the 'space suit'. Operating while having all this equipment on posed an additional challenge. Fortunately, the surgery went well, the patient has been weaned off the ventilator and can now breathe on his own again."

Soma tells me emphatically that wearing masks when going out has been the single most important thing we have done in Singapore to control the spread of the virus. He reminded me that we should not slack in our efforts and we do it not just for ourselves but for our loved ones and others as well.

He believes being a responsible civilian will go a long way. Following the simple steps of wearing masks, social distancing and avoiding unnecessary trips to public places as much as possible will make a difference.

I quickly looked around and took a sip of my coffee, grateful that we are in Phase 2 and can now dine at restaurants and F&B outlets, and masks can be removed when eating or drinking.

I asked: "So what has kept you going all this time?"

It's to come home to his family and interact with his children, said Soma. They give him a completely different perspective to his daily challenges, and this "switch" helps him to maintain a balance.

The other source of motivation for Soma is hearing (and sometimes reading) the words of encouragement and gratitude from patients.

"What do you think of the daily updates on the number of foreign workers infected?" I asked.

His reply surprised me. He said that even though there are new cases reported each day, there are even more workers who have recovered and have gone back to work. Knowing that so many have fought through and survived the virus gave him hope and solace.

It was at this point that I thought to myself, "we will be ok".

It's an odd epiphany. I've always been looking ahead, knowing in my head that the world would recover, once the vaccine is discovered and mass produced, once the economy rebounds from the Covid-19 depression.

But talking to my friend, listening to his personal journey and his quiet sacrifices gave me the confidence in my heart that thanks to him, and many others like him, we will be ok.

Healthcare workers all around the world are on the frontlines of battling Covid-19, stopping it from spreading throughout our cities and into our homes. They are putting themselves in the path of this virus in this unprecedented crisis while sacrificing their livelihoods and even their lives. Our doctors, nurses, Emergency Medical Technicians, transporters, pharmacists and everyone who supports patient care have risen to the occasion and cared for our most vulnerable when needed.

Their dedication, commitment and courage deserve our deepest gratitude and admiration. Their service to patients in saving countless lives and making a difference to many is heroic.

My friend, Dr Soma, a frontliner, is a real hero.

I survived Covid-19, now I want to help others through tough times

Not wanting others to go through what she did, Cobid-19 survivor sets up neighbourhood buddy system to support the lonely, elderly and low-income families.

by Serene Leong

In March 2020, 27-year-old Tan Li Mei was working as a product manager in New York City. Today, she is a Covid-19 survivor in Singapore. Her week in a National University Hospital recovery ward fighting the virus gave her a first-hand perspective of the frontline heroes who tended to patients like her.

She also got a front-seat view of how other victims, many of whom were elderly, suffered alone.

Seeing their difficulties, she was inspired to co-found a ground-up movement called Kampung Kakis to give back to society after her second lease on life.

Says Li Mei: "I wanted to pay forward what our healthcare workers have done for me and make a difference in the community, especially when I think about the elderly who don't have caregivers and other people falling through the cracks."

"I wanted to create a platform where people who need help can find help from someone staying close to them. Hopefully this kampung spirit can extend beyond Covid-19."

Getting Covid

But back in March, things were bleak in New York.

Looking back, Li Mei said she realised that the warning signs had been there. The city was on lockdown. Numbers of the infected were escalating. Businesses were closing. Li Mei's sister urged her to come home because their parents were worried.

She quickly booked a flight back to Singapore but it was too late. Li Mei was already feeling fatigued.

She admits to The Pride: "I would be very tired by 8pm and I would sleep 12 hours a day. A few times when I went for a run or did a workout at home, I got really breathless. But I thought maybe I was unfit."

The day before her flight home, Li Mei developed a sore throat.

After she reached Singapore on March 23, Li Mei started her Stay-Home Notice, taking extra precautions to distance herself safely from her family.

She says: "I tried to be very careful around my parents. I made sure they left my food at my door. Everything [I used to eat] was disposable. I had my own bathroom."

Thankfully, because of these precautions, her parents did not fall ill. But when a few Singaporean friends who were with her in New York tested positive upon returning home, Li Mei decided to get herself tested on March 26.

That was when she discovered she had Covid-19.

Even though her worst fears had come true, Li Mei says that her concerns were unfounded.

During her time at NUH, Li Mei kept friends and family updated through her Instagram stories. *Credit: Tan Li Mei.*

"I was very lucky. The doctors said I was one of the fastest recovering patients!"

If Li Mei had one word to describe her experience in the hospital, it would be "gratitude".

"I've always taken our healthcare system and the quality of our doctors and nurses for granted. Medical workers in NYC are having to raise funds to buy personal protective equipment to protect themselves, while nurses in Singapore change out of their PPEs every time they enter a different isolation ward."

Li Mei adds: "I realised our healthcare professionals are all very compassionate – everyone was very reassuring, telling me not to worry even though I could tell they were very tired."

"The level of attention to detail and amount of care that they give to their patients is so different compared to anywhere else in the world. I felt very thankful to be a Singaporean."

During her stay, family and friends were not allowed to visit, but Li Mei communicated with her parents on WhatsApp regularly to give them updates and put them at ease.

Even though she was away from loved ones, Li Mei formed a bond with four other women in the same Covid treatment ward, who helped each other get through their recovery process.

"We had a little community going on. I was new to the ward and they welcomed me. They helped me feel like I was not alone in this because we were all going through the same thing."

"To keep the morale up, whenever someone got discharged or moved to the recovery facility, we would cheer and congratulate them!"

It wasn't just the patients and the medical personnel who helped her keep her spirits up. Even the staff member who delivered the food every day often brought warmth and cheer to the ward.

Said Li Mei: "The 'uncle' was very funny. If I don't eat my snacks or drink my Milo, he will be like 'eh your Milo turning cold'. [That little act of kindness] made such a big difference."

Li Mei is also thankful that as a young and healthy person, she was able to recover quickly. In the ward across the hall, she had a first-hand view of an elderly Covid sufferer who was not doing as well.

"He was on his bed the whole time looking miserable. One day, his symptoms worsened. The call bell rang constantly. He was vomiting, breathless, and the nurses and doctors were all rushing to him. It was quite hard seeing someone suffer that much from Covid."

"It could have been me. Worse, it could have been my parents," she added soberly.

Helping others through tough times
Seeing elderly patients suffering from the disease and receiving such care from medical workers deeply impacted Li Mei.

Inspired by the kindness she saw in the wards, and galvanised by her personal battle with the disease, Li Mei thought of a neighbourhood buddy system to support the lonely, elderly and low-income families during the pandemic.

Two weeks after her discharge from NUH, Li Mei, with the help of two other millennials, launched Kampung Kakis.

When she reached out to the residents' committees to look for help, Li Mei met Michelle Lau, 26, chairman of her RC. She helped rally other RCs within the Gek Poh Ville community in Jurong, and designed a resource kit for distribution.

Together with Denise Tay, 25, Li Mei's long-time friend with a passion for helping others, the three formed the core team that started Kampung Kakis.

Within its first two weeks, Kampung Kakis received 240 Kaki sign-ups. So far, 11 beneficiaries have been matched with Kakis and they are looking to raise greater awareness to reach more seniors in need of a Kaki.

"Kampung Kakis is as effective as the strength of our network. We match based on proximity and needs. We try to not match anyone beyond a 20-minute walk because we hope that after the circuit breaker ends, they can still be a befriender to their Kaki-in-need," says Li Mei.

Co-founders of Kampung Kakis, from left to right: Li Mei, Denise and Michelle.
Credit: Tan Li Mei.

Credit: Kampung Kakis.

During the circuit breaker, Kakis were advised to stay home as much as possible and to only leave home (while adhering to safe distancing) if they had to assist persons with disabilities or seniors above the age of 60 with their daily needs.

Kakis can also provide help through various ways that don't require physical contact, such as picking up groceries, providing meals, or simply lending a listening ear.

"We are not a social service organisation so we don't fundraise or give out food or monetary help. We encourage our Kakis to help within their own means and if they are not comfortable giving financial assistance, they don't have to do so," says Li Mei.

One of Kampung Kaki's beneficiaries is a 23-year-old single mother with three young children who had lost her job. She recently matched with a Kaki who is helping her find support and resources available from the government.

Another beneficiary, a man who lives alone, was facing stress and anxiety over job fears. Kampung Kakis successfully matched him with a nearby Kaki who has been listening and providing career mentorship.

"Having someone check on you regularly, encouraging you to not give up, helping you to get out of your situation, can make a big difference," Li Mei says.

Currently, Kampung Kakis is looking to improve its model.

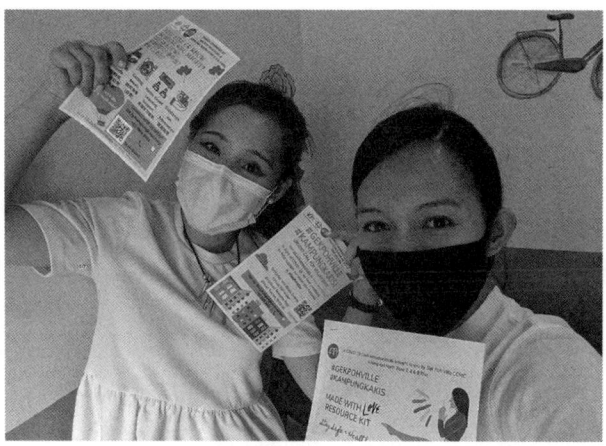

Li Mei and Michelle distributing posters at a mask distribution drive in early April. *Credit: Tan Li Mei.*

Li Mei plans to return to New York when the situation calms down (she is still employed at the same company and working remotely), but she still hopes to continue helping Singaporeans even while in the US.

"No matter what happens, I hope we don't stop serving our community and that we keep growing the team, bringing together people who have the same mindset and passion for helping others, and see where that takes us."

Li Mei says her time in hospital changed how she saw the world.

"Covid gave me a lot of time in the hospital to reflect. When you know this is a deadly disease and you hear about people with mild symptoms today going into ICU the next day, it makes you think."

"I don't want to waste my life. If I had to die tomorrow, [I want to know] what have I done with my life, who have I helped, have I made this world a better place?"

I was stuck overseas after I flew home, away from home

He flew home for his mother's last rites, and Covid-19 turned an already-emotional journey into a quarantine adventure filled with moments of kindness.

by Nava Neminathan

It felt eerie standing next to a solitary vehicle in a deserted parking lot at an international airport past midnight. The harsh floodlights only served to emphasise the vast and empty space around me.

The date was May 6, 2020, and I was at the Bandaranaike International Airport outside Colombo and I was ready to fly home to my wife and son in Singapore.

It had been almost two months since I returned to my hometown in Sri Lanka to perform the last rites for my mum.

The journey to the airport had been sudden and arduous, as the expectation to be able to fly home after a seven-week total lockdown had been non-existent until about 36 hours previously.

When I found out that there was a cargo flight leaving Sri Lanka for Singapore to repatriate Singaporeans stranded in the country, it was go time. But it was a mad scramble trying to liaise on multiple fronts: getting the flight ticket, seeking clearance to travel, arranging for a driver during curfew; not to mention putting my personal affairs in order and my personal belongings into a bag.

The mad scramble on May 5 mirrored my hurried entry into the country in March.

I had always been in regular contact with Mum, who was living with little assistance well into her 80s in our hometown of Trincomalee. So the frantic call from my sister past midnight on March 17 was a shock.

She was crying over the phone while trying to convey the news of Mum's sudden demise but there was no time to mourn. I had 24 hours to fly into Sri Lanka before the airport was closed over Covid-19.

There were so many unknowns: my work responsibilities, the quarantine procedures in Sri Lanka, the funeral arrangements... but one thing was for sure. I knew that the moment I landed in Colombo, I wouldn't be able to return to Singapore for a long time.

I think it is ironic that both my journey to Sri Lanka and my travel back home to Singapore were hurried breathless affairs, but both trips, not to mention my stay in Sri Lanka, were filled with moments of gratefulness.

Landing in Colombo in the wee hours of March 19 was surreal as I walked through a quiet airport with empty aisles and shuttered duty-free shops. Little did I know that in seven weeks, I would be flying out of the country in similar fashion!

But in March, I was worried, stressed and sleep-deprived. After touching down, I still had to reach my hometown 200km away before the morning was over. Fortunately, my aunt and cousin in Colombo picked me up at that ungodly hour and drove directly to my hometown, with wreaths and garlands in tow!

The sun was rising as I reached Mum's home and I was finally able to relax and get a quick rest before performing her last rites. Despite the threat of Covid-19 and resulting limitations on public gatherings, it was a sense of relief to be able to conclude the religious rituals before curfew was imposed on the entire island on March 20.

Mum had been put to rest. But I was stuck in Sri Lanka.

Deserted streets in Trincomalee.
Credit: Navaneethan Neminathan

Experiencing a Sri Lankan "circuit breaker"

Thus began the days of emptiness and uncertainty as no family or friend could visit us during our mourning period. It was just my sister, myself and a helper who was also dealing with the shock of Mum's sudden demise.

I had taken leave to go to Sri Lanka, but with no return in sight. I could not stay on leave indefinitely. So when the curfew was lifted the following week, on two days for about eight hours, my priority was to get wifi installed so as to connect to the outside world and work. Around me, many of my neighbours were stocking up (just as in Singapore) on goods, both the essential and frivolous.

So even before Singapore started its circuit breaker, I was already working from home – my Sri Lankan home, that is.

My WFH experience had to be one of the furthest commutes from my office at Stamford Court, in Singapore!

Even though I was thousands of miles away, I was grateful to be able to work because, being stranded with no inkling of a return date, it allowed me a routine that kept me sane.

My life became structured as never before, as I embraced the routine of telecommuting where work was interspersed with breaks for physical activity and meals.

Night-time was mainly spent watching the news on TV, followed by chatting with family and friends on the phone (Sri Lanka is two and half hours behind Singapore).

Left: The view from inside my house in Trincomalee. Three layers of locks separate me from the outside world. Right: My walled-off garden, where I could take a breather from work. *Credit: Nava Neminathan.*

Watching the news every night, I was troubled by the sufferings of daily wage earners who couldn't even get a square meal, while much of the food being produced by the already-poor farmers was going to waste because of Covid-related disruptions to transport and distribution networks.

I was immensely grateful for having a roof above my head, with a supply of food and utilities that enabled a comfortable, almost-normal life, while so many lives were being overturned by the coronavirus.

At times I felt guilty of my privilege and also frustrated by my inability to make a difference to those in need, due to my unfamiliarity with my surroundings and my limited social network.

I felt like a prisoner in my own home and a stranger in my own country.

Adding to that was the undercurrent of grief that I still had to deal with over Mum's passing. In the end, I sought solace in my daily routine and focused on the cultural and religious responsibilities I had to do related to Mum's death in order to keep myself going.

But I wasn't the only one dealing with loneliness. My wife and son were concerned about how long I had to stay away, and soon "what can be done towards your coming home?" became the focus of our daily conversations.

Repatriation from my nation home to my adopted home was something I had not thought about and I missed several opportunities to return to Singapore as a result of not having registered with the consulate in Sri Lanka.

So I joined the few Singaporeans left behind, biding our time until the authorities of both countries could synchronise their efforts to make it worth coordinating a flight home for us!

Liaising with diplomats and bureaucrats at ministries and high commissions, not to mention disoriented airlines staff, just to secure a seat on the repatriation flight was a feat in itself.

I will always be grateful to those who worked tirelessly beyond the call of duty to make that happen.

Those were the thoughts running through my mind as I stood alone under the glaring white floodlights in the car park outside Bandaranaike International Airport on May 6.

I couldn't enter the airport terminal early because operations were limited due to Covid-19 restrictions. But even on the cusp of returning to Singapore, I was still receiving kindness, this time from my driver who decided to keep me company and ensure that I was allowed into the airport before he returned home.

It felt strange to be the sole person inside a darkened terminal. I had the waiting lounge all to myself, but waiting for the skeleton staff to clear me for boarding didn't allow for much rest. I wasn't worried though, I knew I would get some well-needed rest after boarding.

It was unreal to be the only passenger seated on an entire row and not have a blanket for warmth, due to Covid-19 related flying restrictions. But I was still thankful for being given a hot meal and a 1.5 litre bottle of water – all at one go though, so as to minimise contact between crew and passengers!

My journey of gratitude came full circle after touching down at Changi International Airport, and I was relieved despite not knowing what was in store for me.

But it didn't matter. I was in Singapore, finally. I was back on the same soil as my family and my spirits were lifted. That wasn't the end of my adventure though. I still had 14 days of isolation to endure, but that will be a tale for another time!

My Stay-Home Notice in a five-star hotel showed me a different side to myself

After returning from Sri Lanka, I served my Stay-Home Notice at the Shangri-La's Rasa Sentosa Resort & Spa and discovered a new way of looking at solitude.

by Nava Neminathan

I was on a bus. In Singapore. Finally.

After a 20-hour journey for a trip that normally takes eight hours, I was home, back on safe (and predictable) soil.

But I didn't know where I was going.

It was May 6, 2020, and I was one of nine passengers who returned on a flight from Sri Lanka. It was the middle of the day, in the middle of the circuit breaker, and I was groggy and disoriented, having not slept since I was whisked away from my hometown in Trincomalee.

I was still experiencing a mix of disbelief and relief at being able to get a flight back to Singapore after having waited for weeks.

I had hoped to be told about what lay ahead – the flight crew kept to themselves – at immigration or after clearing it, but was simply waved out of the arrival hall to a parking bay and into one of the waiting buses.

There was no exchange of pleasantries, just a passport check, health declaration and temperature taking. I asked the driver if I could go back into the airport to withdraw some cash from an ATM machine.

"Do it at the hotel," he said without elaborating.

After waiting for a few more passengers (just four in a 40-seater), the bus exited the terminal and entered the beautifully landscaped ECP. I couldn't resist asking the person sitting in front with the driver as to where we were going.

He grunted out a single word.

I was going to Sentosa.

Arriving at Shangri-La

Even though I've lived in Singapore for 20 years, I had only visited Sentosa to take visitors to the laser show, S.E.A. Aquarium and Universal Studios Singapore. I didn't realise Sentosa was more than just these attractions until the bus reached Shangri-La's Rasa Sentosa Resort and Spa.

My only concern was having to survive 14 days in a closed air-conditioned environment after the open air and sunshine of Sri Lanka, especially as I have sinusitis and an aversion to cold and tight living conditions.

However, I was reluctant to ask anything as I was uncomfortable with the luxury and opulence of a swanky five-star hotel.

We were welcomed at the counter with a box of pretzels and a request for our credit cards, for a deposit that would be refunded on checkout.

As we were led to our rooms, I carried my luggage. It was my first indication of what was to come. We were coming from the lands of the infected, after all, to be excluded and observed.

So close, yet so far away. *Credit: Nava Neminathan.*

The greatest relief I had upon entering Room 723 was seeing the balcony, not for its beautiful view of the sea, but the realisation that I could breathe fresh air.

My fears about coming down with allergic rhinitis prompting a Covid misdiagnosis evaporated when I opened the balcony doors to invite the warmth and sea breeze into the room.

After a shower, a snack and a nap, I was awakened by the doorbell. I drew my curtains to see the sun setting, then opened the door to see a package left on a stool. Peering out into the empty corridor, I saw that each room had a stool outside on which food packs and drink cans were placed.

It was then that I realised we weren't allowed to meet anyone – we had to bring in the food left at the door, clean up after ourselves, then leave our garbage outside to be disposed of.

I had become an untouchable.

Life in a room that I was not allowed to step out of

I had all my meals at the balcony under the sun and the moon, feeling the sea breeze (and the rain!). My greatest discovery was that when the balcony doors were open, the air-conditioning would switch off. For 14 nights, I slept with the balcony doors ajar.

I was concerned about food, not over its quality but its quantity. There was too much of it! For example, for my first meal on arrival, I received a vegetarian bento dinner packed to the brim with pasta, salad, dessert and juice.

For a small eater like me who hates wasting food, it took me till midnight to finish it. I couldn't waste any of the five-star efforts from the hotel's kitchen staff!

The next morning, at 6am, I opened the door to see breakfast on the stool (the doorbell woke me up). Jet-lagged and sleep-deprived, I left it there and went back to bed.

Yes, breakfast had been left outside the door before 7am for someone who usually has coffee only at 9am and a slice of bread after 11am.

When I finally got to the breakfast, cold after being left out for a few hours, I realised that it included noodles, juice and fruit – enough for lunch, which was going to be served soon!

In my desperation to avoid wasting food, I called reception, and was directed to room service.

"Sorry, sir, you want what again? Less food? And no, I'm sorry, we can't give you a kids' meal because we don't have a vegetarian option."

Strange requests

The one who took my call must have found my request strange. In the end, I asked for the Indian vegetarian option, hoping for a smaller portion.

Later, I called room service again to ask them to send only fruits for dinner as I was still eating lunch – I wasn't going to have it thrown away! The bizarre requests from Room 723 must have reached someone important because I received a call from a chef the next day.

While explaining my concerns about food wastage to the chef and asking for smaller portions for all my meals, I realised that he was a fellow Indian, a Tamil-speaker. It made it easier for me to convey my food concerns and ask for something light for breakfast and dinner.

After that first odd conversation, the chef and I built an affinity. I spoke with Pradeep almost daily, and he took care of my meals. He even let me know of his days off, so that I would be prepared for the extra food (which I kept in the mini-fridge). I even learnt to warm the food for later, by using steam from the kettle!

As the days went by, I replaced the breakfast juice with a packet of milk and used it for my coffee and tea – no powdered creamer for me! It was a process of learning and making small discoveries each day, to keep myself engaged.

I know it sounds a little picky and I am certainly not complaining about my stay.

It's just to illustrate that being left alone without physical human interaction for 14 days can take a toll on anyone (my only contact came from random spot-checks by SHN officers), and it became important to be able to control what I could – large or small – within my environment.

Room self-service

My other concern was cleaning.

Cleaning up the room, with an open balcony door! *Credit: Nava Neminathan.*

I was given new towels twice a week and bed linen weekly, with free laundry service of up to four items per day. I started wondering what the hotel would do with the linen!

When it became clear that no one was going to clean my room, I asked for cleaning equipment. It seemed like I was being an oddity again as not many guests had done that – housekeeping sent me rags (made from towels) to wipe the floors instead of brooms or mops!

Dust was a problem, thanks to my open balcony door. Thankfully, after several requests, I secured a small broom and dustpan. It was a triumphant moment. Between that, and being able to wash both the bathroom and balcony, I was good.

Washing the balcony was crucial, since I often shared meals there with feathered friends, who would inadvertently leave some "gifts" behind. Nonetheless, it was a treat to have them come and perch fearlessly on the balcony rails during my mealtimes.

Working from hotel

Within a day of returning, I started my own WFH (work-from-hotel) routine. With the help of good wifi, I took my colleagues on a virtual tour of the room! That was when I realised that they would swap places with me in a heartbeat! They even teased me for "promoting the hotel" with all the photos I was sending them.

That was when I started appreciating the circumstances of my SHN.

Sentosa sounds like *santhosam* in Tamil, which means "happiness". And I learnt that my guess wasn't far off, since Sentosa translates as "peace and tranquility" in Malay, which is in turn derived from the Sanskrit term *santosha*.

I learnt that piece of trivia during the weekly quizzes hosted by comedian Hossan Leong and organised by the guest relations team. We had daily virtual yoga and zumba sessions too.

Between working during the day and catching up with TV and phone calls at night, I stopped feeling so trapped.

Despite being on the seventh floor, I felt close to nature, with the sun and moon shining directly on the balcony and the wind and rain being welcome companions.

I began to appreciate tracking the full moon as it moved across the sky, playing hide-and-seek from behind the clouds. On rainy days, it was a pleasure watching the sun follow the same pattern too.

I became more attuned to the sounds of nature, realised that the screeches in the mornings came from the family of peacocks roaming the garden below and not calls from monkeys in nearby trees.

The other rooms began to fill up as more Singaporeans came home. I started to see more people making use of their balconies, to work, exercise or simply take in the sights. We would wave at each other and exchange pleasantries.

On the 13th day of my Stay-Home Notice, a letter arrived with checkout details. I was "graduating" from my SHN (I actually received a certificate from Shangri-La!) at the Rasa Sentosa.

Left: I spent many evenings watching the moon move across the sky. Right: It became my hobby to take photos of the visiting birds to share with friends and family. *Credit: Nava Neminathan.*

Taking in the sunset with a neighbour. *Credit: Nava Neminathan.*

A sweet treat waiting for me when I got home. And a certificate indicating that I had completed my SHN at the Rasa Sentosa. *Credit: Nava Neminathan.*

Everything had been meticulously taken care of, including the collection of unused, non-perishable food (which I had plenty of) for donation to a food bank.

At checkout, I signed, smiled and thanked the staff for taking care of me. Pradeep wasn't there but I had already thanked him over the phone.

I was impressed by how the staff and management had handled us. We were not willing guests, and we were uncertain and fearful. They went the extra mile to assuage our concerns and show care for our physical and mental wellbeing.

Despite being alone for two weeks, I was in no mood to chat with the driver taking me away from Sentosa, as I was lost in thoughts of my short stay.

Those two weeks taught me to appreciate a different world view – that there can be simplicity in luxury. And kindness in every moment.

Appreciating those who serve

It has been over seven months since my stay at the Rasa Sentosa, and since then, there have been many other stories of Singaporeans sharing their experiences – both good and bad.

The hotel itself has re-opened to visitors. Nowadays, its rooms are filled with Singaporeans rediscovering the joys of staycations and luxe hotel living.

Despite Covid-19 still raging in many parts of the world, we have remained relatively safe within Singapore. We should commend those tireless frontline heroes, including hospitality staff, for sacrificing their time and efforts to make our lives better.

Even as we deal with the challenges of the new normal, we in Singapore should be thankful for what we have. And to view our situation in the right perspective.

Covid-19: How I survived a 14-day Stay-Home Notice

In the early days of Covid-19, when we were still finding out about the pandemic, one Singaporean writes about her SHN experience.

by Faith Lee

Today (April 2, 2020) is my first day back at the office after a 14-day mandatory Stay-Home Notice (SHN), also known to many Singaporeans as "cannot leave home".

Although 14 days is a short time, with so much happening outside, it felt like an eternity.

This is my story.

Fifteen days ago, I arrived back in Singapore from Malaysia, a country deemed to be at a high risk of exposure to Covid-19.

Singapore had just announced a wave of border restrictions, where all travellers, including Singapore residents who had travelled to ASEAN countries, UK, Japan and Switzerland, were to be issued a 14-day SHN.

When the news broke on the evening of March 15, my night was spent replying to texts from concerned relatives, friends and colleagues asking me if I would be able to book a flight back the next day to "beat the clock".

It seemed like there were many clocks to beat because right after that came the news

Pasta, the best alternative to instant noodles. *Credit: Faith Lee.*

that Malaysia would implement its Movement Control Order (MCO) from March 18. A second surge of texts came asking me to leave the country before it went into effect.

Well, I was on a flight back to Singapore on the day the MCO started.

For those who may not yet know the details, a SHN is different from a Quarantine Order (QO) or a Leave of Absence (LOA). In a SHN, I am not allowed out of my place of residence, even if I need essentials such as food; I had to make my own arrangements. Those who are on quarantine have essentials provided for them while people on LOA could pop out for a bit to grab them. What I was going through was essentially home detention, but without legal charges against me. That being said, I could potentially face legal consequences if I breached it. It is that serious.

Contrary to what some people may think, I did not have the luxury of staying in a hotel with a city or sea view. These were only reserved for returning Singapore residents travelling from the UK or US from March 24.

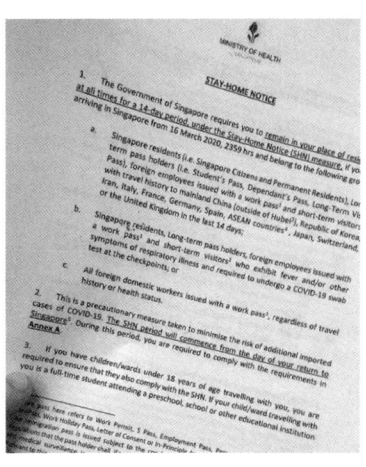

Receiving the SHN from immigration officers. *Credit: Faith Lee.*

Proving myself for the next 14 days

While I waited to see what was in store for me upon landing in Singapore, countless thoughts ran through my mind.

It was the first time I truly felt uncertainty, confusion and guilt during the pandemic. Even though Covid-19 has been in the forefront of everyone's thoughts, this was the first time it truly hit home personally.

Even though I left Singapore before the official travel advisory was announced, would people see me as irresponsible and inconsiderate for travelling during this period of uncertainty? What would my employer say? Would I be required to use my annual leave to cover my absence from the office during the 14 days?

While many did not voice out their opinions directly, it definitely felt like it was me against the world at that point in time; I truly felt the sting of loneliness in self-isolation.

I felt a strong need to prove to others that I was not going to be a statistic and that I was still able to perform my duties while working from home (WFH).

I gave myself two main goals over the next two weeks. First, to make sure that I did not fall sick or develop a fever. Second, to be more responsive and attentive to office matters while working from home. This came at a time when there was a surge in imported cases and companies were still trying to get WFH protocols in place.

Temptations aplenty

Day 0, the day I landed in Singapore, was uneventful. I researched what I needed to do during my SHN and waited for someone to contact me with instructions on what was expected of me. None came. It was only on Day 1 that I got a text from the authorities telling me to report my location via GPS tracking on my mobile phone. Subsequently, these texts started coming two to three times a day at regular intervals.

I was also informed that officials would come by unannounced to check on me and that I would be required to submit a photo of myself and my surroundings. While the officials never came, requests for photos started coming in after about a week into my SHN.

I am a homebody, but I also love taking strolls around the neighbourhood, especially at the NTUC Xtra just opposite where I live. Since the reporting was done via the GPS function on my mobile phone, I thought there could be pockets of time where I could sneak out to the supermarket and foodcourt to grab some supplies and a meal. After days spent within the four walls of my home, the temptation was REAL. It was so enticing, I even gave it a codename: Operation Silent.

After some calculations, I determined that Operation Silent's success rate would be almost 100% if no one knew about it. Thankfully, I came to my senses and aborted the plan. I figured the risks and consequences were simply not worth it. If I was reported and caught, I could face a fine of up to $10,000 or be jailed for up to six months, or both. Lastly, and most importantly, how could I

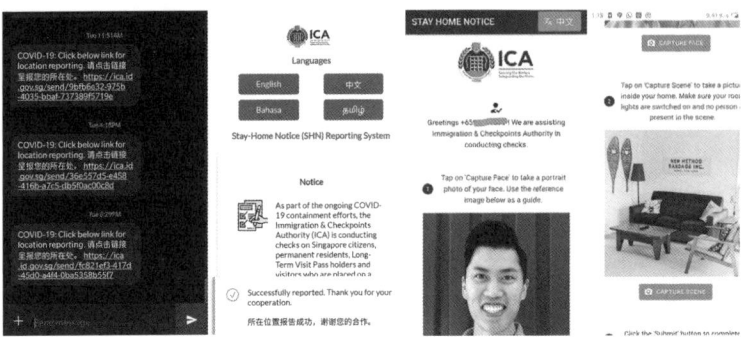

Left: Texts from ICA for location reporting. Right: Example of the submission of photo evidence that I was at home. *Credit: Faith Lee.*

deal with the guilt if I were ill and by going out, put others around me at risk of catching the virus?

A few days after I aborted Operation Silent, it was reported that several people were under investigation for breaching their SHNs. One man allegedly went out for *bak kut teh* upon returning from Myanmar and another had his passport cancelled after ignoring his SHN upon returning from Indonesia. These two cases served as a warning to show just how serious SHNs should be taken.

Physically distant, but socially connected

While that was happening, I had to deal with another growing concern. My supplies were running out. Before this, I never had to worry about food or going hungry. Never did I imagine the day would come when this concern would become a reality for me. I stay with family, but no one cooks, and during the day, everyone is out at work.

Granted, there are food delivery options, but I didn't like the idea of paying a $4 delivery fee just to eat a $5 plate of chicken rice that I can get with a 5-minute walk.

"*Aiyah*, no choice lah, you just gotta do it," was the response some gave. But many know that I'm stubborn.

What I did not expect was how family, friends, colleagues and even ex-interns started reaching out to me, offering to get needed essentials. I was really touched by their kind gestures and accepted some offers for help from those who lived nearer to me. They would buy the items and leave them at my doorstep for me to pick up when they were a safe distance away.

Technology helped to curb the loneliness. I was able to stay connected to people I cared about. Video calls became my favourite mode of communication as I could see who I was talking to.

As I bid farewell to my 14 days of SHN, I started thinking: with Covid-19, would life ever go back to what it used to be?

Probably not.

Working from home while on SHN has got me used to the "new normal" of what is to come. My organisation has just implemented full telecommuting. This means I'm going to have to get used to working from home more now. Although there are inconveniences, I'm not complaining. Working from home has its advantages, such as waking up at 8.50am to start work at 9am. I've not been this punctual in recent months and being able to save time and money on commuting is a welcome benefit.

A humbling experience

There are some lessons that I took away from my experience.

First, being socially responsible is a serious matter. This means ensuring that we keep ourselves safe and healthy to protect those around us, especially the vulnerable. Although I do not have anyone in my household who is particularly vulnerable, it does not mean that I can proceed with life as normal.

My SHN experience has shown me that the government trusts us. It could have opted for a more heavy-handed and draconian approach but I'm glad that the leadership has chosen to put its faith in the honesty and public spiritedness of Singaporeans.

Second, small gestures mean a great deal. Being put in a situation where I had to depend on others to help me with basic needs made this fact very clear to me. Freedom of movement is something that I have always taken for granted. But another thing that I have taken for granted is the daily acts of kindness from people around me.

It has been ingrained in me from a young age to thank people for helping me, but this period has taught me to be more mindful and take more effort in showing appreciation to those who extend a helping hand.

Third, self-care is important. Use the time to improve your well-being and state of mind. I'm not gonna lie. The first few days were tough. The pressure I gave myself to prove my worth took its toll.

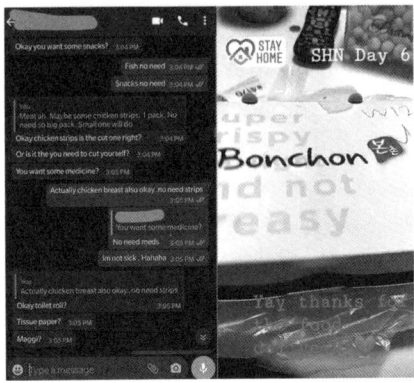 

Left: Friends offering help with the delivery of food. Right: Finally back in office when most are working from home. *Credit: Faith Lee.*

However, as the days passed, these pressures mattered less. People who reached out showed me that there is still room to care in a time like this. I also dedicated 30 minutes daily to work out, something that I had not managed to do in a long time.

We are all in it together

While I was cooped up at home, I was still able to keep up with news. Things around Singapore are looking vastly different, with markers on seats at food establishments and snaking queues but empty malls. But take heart, this will pass.

To all those who are currently serving your SHN, you will get through this. Take this time to connect with others and be kind, especially to yourself. Help is always close by, you just have to ask.

To people who have friends serving SHN, offer help and show care for them. This is the time where your presence means a lot to them.

Safe distancing means staying further from each other physically in the next few weeks or months, but that doesn't mean we should stay socially isolated. Make up for it by caring for each other more as we are all in this fight against Covid-19 together.

"No one is really safe until all of us are safe"

It's official. Phase 3 starts on Dec 28, 2020. But as restrictions get lifted, let's not forget others in our haste to get ahead.

by Solomon Lim

Listening to yesterday's announcement about Phase 3, it wasn't much that we weren't already expecting.

Over the past few weeks, months even, we have been flirting with news of Phase 3 and so PM Lee's address yesterday (Dec 14) didn't bring any earth-shattering news, just confirmation of what we've already been hoping for.

Don't get me wrong. It certainly felt good listening to our leaders tell us how far we've come. From the fears and uncertainty in March and April, through our concerns over our health, our jobs and the economy, we have emerged more hopeful.

The uncertainty remains – the battle is "far from won", warns Mr Lee, as the pandemic still rages in parts of the world – but our fears have gone.

It's a great morale boost to finally put a date – Dec 28 – to Phase 3.

That, coupled with the news that Singapore has secured enough vaccines for everyone on our sunny island by the end of the next year, means that it's looking like a very merry Christmas indeed.

Oddly, the thing that really struck me from yesterday's announcement came not from Mr Lee, but from Manpower Minister Tan See Leng.

He was talking about the measures that Singapore was putting in place for migrant workers in the coming year and ended his press conference segment with a plea to stay the course.

Dr Tan said: "No one is really safe until all of us are safe."

This truism sounds stark and a little depressing, and hearing it made me pause for thought.

Reaching out to migrant workers

Covid has highlighted some of the inequalities within our society. One of the biggest groups of people "hiding in plain sight" in Singapore is our migrant worker community. The pandemic has shown how most Singaporeans, myself included, have taken this group so critical to our nation-building for granted.

Hearing how our migrant worker friends can return to the community in a pilot programme from next year is positive news. Already, some have moved to Quick Build Dorms, a much-needed improvement over their poor standards of living before Covid-19 shone a light on the situation.

Yet there is always room for improvement.

I am ashamed to admit that I didn't know migrant workers are still only permitted to leave their dormitories for work, errands and to visit recreation centres. Even within their dorms, they are subject to many restrictions.

Remember when we went through the circuit breaker? Suffered the cabin fever that made some Singaporeans go off the deep end of frustration and self-centredness? Well, as of the time of this writing, those in the dormitories are still dealing with restrictions

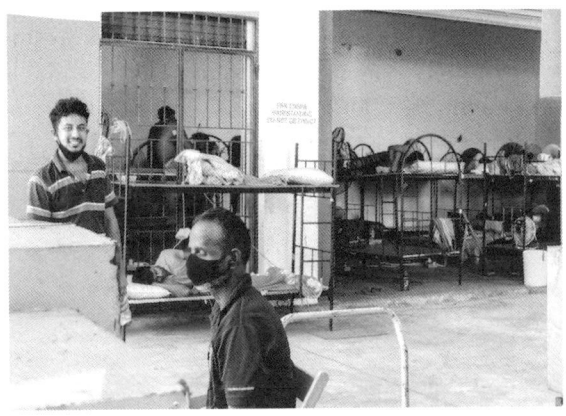

Workers cooped up in poor living conditions. *Credit: Samuel Lim.*

such as having no access to communal cooking facilities, sports and recreation options.

While Singaporeans complain about having to wait for hours to check in for their hotel staycations purchased with SingapoRediscover vouchers, or about how the travel bubble to Hong Kong has been delayed, our migrant worker friends have been stoically staying in their dorms, subject to bi-weekly testing – going out only to work and returning to their bunks only to rest.

It's Raining Raincoats founder Dipa Swaminathan tells The Pride: "Yesterday's news doesn't change much for the migrant workers. A lot of their movements are still restricted. Our migrant workers are making a lot of sacrifices so we can be safe."

"The important thing to bear in mind is that they are human beings just like us. They are alone here, and their families are back home. And they are still among the lowest paid among us. That's a terrible triple whammy."

"Everyone should still do what they can to help. From whatever walk of life you are in, show some compassion."

As part of its continuing outreach to the migrant workers, It's Raining Raincoats is organising events such as bus tours for workers to see the Christmas lights, as well as food and gift giveaways.

Samuel Lim, who works with Hope Initiative Alliance (HIA), says: "We see [migrant workers] a few times a week. HIA works with our adopted dorms to take some workers out on MOM-approved outings to parks for some fresh air."

Migrant workers on an activity organised by It's Raining Raincoats. *Credit: Facebook / Itsrainingraincoats.*

Out on a MOM-approved outing. *Credit: Facebook / Hope Initiative Alliance.*

He adds: "Despite all the restrictions put on them, these workers are really full of gratitude. On an individual level, they're extremely appreciative. What surprises me over and over again is how there isn't a bitter bone in any of them regarding their situation."

For the Christmas period, HIA has organised some ways for members of the public to spread some cheer to migrant workers.

Not just migrant workers, but our neighbours too

Just like one of Covid's silver linings is to shed light on the lives of our migrant workers, another is the opportunity for Singaporeans to spread care and concern for their neighbours.

Over the past months, we have seen how Singaporeans have come together to support one another. Of course, this wasn't the case at first, when our *kiasu* and *kiasi* compatriots cleared supermarket shelves in a flurry of panic buying.

But when cooler heads and warmer hearts prevailed, we saw many stories of people reaching out to help their fellows.

We've heard of Singaporeans contributing their Solidarity payments, singing in virtual choirs and handing out free sanitisers and masks.

Some, inspired by their own experiences, have set up movements to help the needy, like Kampung Kaki's Tan Li Mei, a Covid-19 survivor who wanted to pay forward what healthcare workers did for her. She and her volunteers have helped Singaporeans who have been hurting, and not just due to Covid, such as a father and daughter duo who had to deal with multiple personal tragedies over the years.

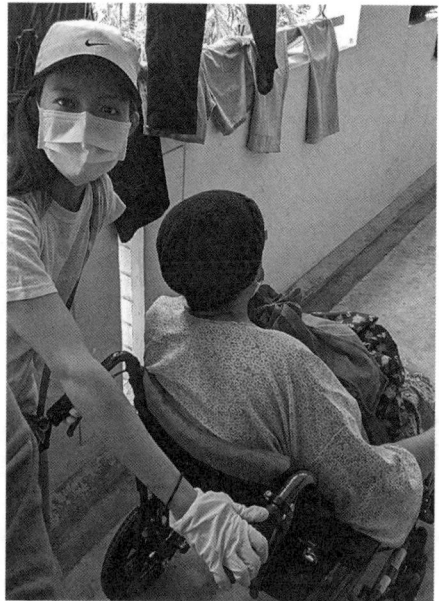

Tan Li Mei with one of the beneficiaries of the Kampung Kakis programme. *Credit: Tan Li Mei.*

And Kampung Kaki is just one of the very many ground-up movements that have sprung up this year.

Finding kindness in Covid

In many ways, Covid has increased the distance between people. We keep strangers at arms' length. We are faceless behind the ubiquitous masks that we have to put on. We are reduced to nameless numbers linked by our TraceTogether apps.

Yet ask yourself this: Have you become kinder after Covid as compared to before?

Call me an idealist but I daresay we have. It is when something comes under threat, that we cherish it a bit more.

Covid has forced us to slow down, and somewhere along the way, we have learnt to smell the roses.

We've learnt to be kind to our neighbours, reach out to our families and be more attentive to our friends.

Yes, we have all struggled with our darker periods, through mental wellness issues, especially when having to deal with the challenges of our new normal.

But we aren't alone. And if you don't already know that, I'm reminding you of it now.

So how do we ensure that we continue to cherish each other? There has been talk of herd immunity against Covid. The jury is still out on that, but suffice it to say, it's not looking feasible without working together with a vaccine.

So let's practise a new kind of herd behaviour. One that looks after each other. In nature, the herd looks after its members. There is safety in numbers, with the stronger members looking out for the young and the frail.

We are already practising this herd behaviour. Via ground-up movements and volunteer organisations, in caring for our loved ones and through interactions with those around us, we are looking after our own.

"No one is really safe until all of us are safe." Dr Tan's words are stark. Yet they cheered me up.

That's because with one simple sentence, Dr Tan suggested what we should all aspire towards – to be greater. He treated everyone in Singapore as compatriots, regardless of race, religion, culture or ethnicity.

There was no "them" in his statement. There is only "us".

To quote one of my daughter's favourite songs: "We're all in this together."

As we look into Phase 3 and beyond, in 2021 and after, let's not forget about the lessons of kindness we have learnt this year. We've been taught them at a cost, and the battle is still not won.

But we know which side we're on. The same side, together.

I got married during Covid-19 and it was everything I expected... and not

Despite the restrictions and setbacks, getting married during Covid was a chance to share the joy and kindness with friends, family and even strangers!

by Chee Wen Qi

Getting married this year was a challenge.

Like many other couples who decided to tie the knot in 2020, Covid-19 took us by surprise.

While some other couples postponed their nuptials due to the restrictions caused by the pandemic, my husband and I decided to go ahead with our plans.

We had to work with the limited number of guests and that challenge made us cherish every single person we had at our wedding.

Despite not being able to go ahead with our original plans of celebrating our joy with the many friends and family members on our invitation list, my Covid wedding became a reminder of all the acts of kindness from people around me.

Kindness in blessings received

Paring down our guest list was the biggest challenge for us.

Both my husband and I have rather large extended families and so we agonised over how to give the bad news to those who were looking forward to attending the ceremony.

Yet, when the time came, the understanding shown by my relatives touched me greatly.

Instead of grousing over pecking order, they were all willing to give up more slots so that I could invite other guests. In the end, most of my parents' siblings sent two representatives per family

Friends and relatives Zooming in for our wedding. *Credit: Chee Wen Qi.*

to share our joy in person and those who could not attend were still there in spirit – sending gifts and well-wishes to us on the big day itself.

We could do this because, in true working-from-home fashion, we had set up a Zoom meeting for our wedding! That was how many of our close friends and relatives got to see us exchange our vows.

In fact, having our ceremony broadcast online actually gave extended relatives who live overseas the chance of seeing us get married in real time!

Not being able to see many of my friends in person on my big day really made me realise how important it is to be able to give and receive a blessing from others and helped me truly look forward to meeting my loved ones again when restrictions are relaxed.

Kindness in help rendered

Since wedding professionals added to the headcount allowed for the wedding, many of my close friends and cousins volunteered their services for us, just so that they could be there!

The emcee, the decorations and setup, even the photography, videography and editing, were all "internally sourced" which made it all seem so much more intimate.

I may not have had a grand wedding of 40 or 50 tables but seeing my loved ones spontaneously stepping up with whatever skills and abilities they had made me feel as if my ceremony was a personal project for them.

It wasn't professional, but it was perfect. I wouldn't have wanted it any other way.

Kindness in loved ones reconnected

My November wedding also gave me the opportunity to reconnect with my relatives. As with most big families, Chinese New Year is when we get together and update one another on our lives.

This year especially, many of us haven't had the chance to reach out, being concerned with our careers and our health or simply trying to weather the Covid storm.

Our wedding gave me a chance to reach out again, even if it was only to apologise for not being able to invite them.

Ironically, it was during those conversations that I started reconnecting at a deeper level with my cousins. We reminisced about the past, laughed about the times when we were partners in crime, doing silly and fun stuff in our childhood days.

Older cousins would tell me how they couldn't believe how their "little sister" (I was one of the babies of the family) is actually getting married and moving on to another stage of life!

Imagine how good it felt to have a wedding rejection text turn into a happy catch-up session!

My aunties also started texting me (so much more tech-savvy now that mobile phones have become one of the main ways of staying

One of my tech-savvy aunties. *Credit: Chee Wen Qi.*

in touch), reminding me not to be too stressed over the wedding planning and to focus on being beautiful and happy!

One dear aunt told me something that stuck with me throughout all the ups-and-downs of the wedding planning journey: "It is about the both of you. Just be happy. That is what matters."

Kindness in gracious gestures

Covid aside, what do you think is one of the worst things that could possibly happen on your wedding day?

Yep, you got that right. Just minutes before I was going to leave home for the ceremony, I discovered a tear in my wedding gown. I sound calm now, telling the story, but I certainly wasn't in the best state that day!

Cutting the story short, I did whatever I could to fix it but not being a seamstress, I ended up using my veil and very specific body postures to try to hide the rip!

After surviving the wedding day, my husband and I gave our feedback to the bridal boutique and we were pleasantly surprised by their kindness.

Not only did they not charge me for the damage, they refunded the rental fee! The owner even apologised because she thought that she had ruined my big day. Her gracious behaviour defused a potentially ugly dispute.

And it wasn't just her. My husband and I were surprised at the graciousness and flexibility from all the vendors we engaged for our wedding over the changing of plans due to the pandemic.

Kindness from strangers in the community

Did these succulents catch your eye? Cacti isn't exactly your standard wedding favour, but it still warmed my heart when our vendor presented it to my husband when he went to collect our favours.

They didn't have to do it, and it is an expense in lean times like these. Yet that little kind gesture – of helping us "plant love" – made us appreciate how they were happy to share our joy.

Thinking back on my wedding planning journey, I must say I felt like everyone was sharing our joy. I know it sounds silly (I mean, of course weddings are meant to be joyful!), but somehow it felt like my marriage gave people around us an additional reason to show

A cactus gift for our guests. *Credit: Chee Wen Qi.*

kindness and shower love on each other during our gloomiest times.

Even the public Telegram wedding chat channels that we subscribed to in preparation for our wedding were wholesome and supportive.

Reading those chats just affirmed how helpful Singaporeans can be. We were strangers, yet we were sharing suggestions and giving feedback just so that all of us who were getting married could get the best deal or find the right solutions.

It made me reflect on how we should not take happy milestones such as getting married or having a child for granted. Hearing of someone getting married may not be surprising or new but each person experiences this same milestone differently. It is a journey that only they can go through.

So it helps to look beyond our own personal pursuits and help where we can so that another person can have a better day. In expanding my heart, I am reminded of the importance of sharing the joy of others as well.

I am glad to have celebrated this life milestone with the people who matter and humbled to have learnt how our humanity binds us together.

And that's the greatest gift (aside from my husband of course!) that I took away from my Covid wedding.

Finding mental wellness

Covid-19 made me relive my years of struggling with depression

I isolated myself because I was already feeling disconnected from everyone else.

by Nicole K

I was a clumsy kid.

I don't recall a period where I wasn't either nursing a bleeding knee or a swollen ankle. I sprained my ankles so often that I could pinpoint the severity of the sprain just by looking at the colour of the veins around the site of the swell.

This cycle of instability started when I was walking along a narrow footpath and my foot slipped off an insignificant one-inch drop between concrete and grass. My left ankle doubled in size and my father, a traditional Chinese man who believed in no pain, no gain, took 17-year-old me to see the *sinseh*.

At the TCM hall, I remembered being intrigued by this ancient-looking scale which was a wooden beam balanced by a weight on one end and a pan of herbs on the other.

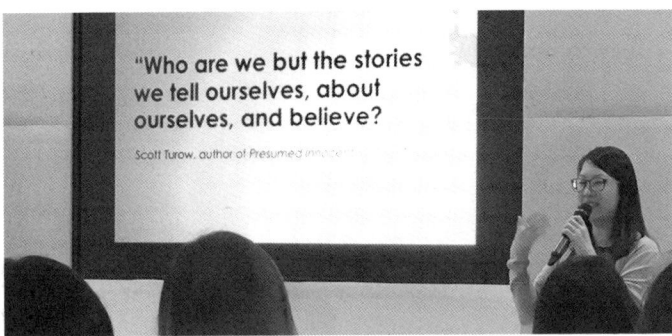

Nicole at one of her talks. *Credit: Nicole K.*

Like that medicinal scale, our mental health shifts and pivots according to the weights of our biology and biography – a confluence of external circumstances and life events.

During the circuit breaker, many of us were forced to reckon with a world tilted on its head, thrown off-kilter by Covid-19 and its effects. In this new normal, what happens when we are displaced from our usual routines and contexts? What do we do when the lines between work and play converge? And how do we meaningfully connect with one another with social distancing measures?

Mental health is intrinsically tied to our sense of self. Our mental state colours the way we perceive the world, the way we relate to others, and how we determine meaning and self-worth. Therefore, in a desperate attempt to recalibrate our sense of self, we grasp at the unravelling strands of normalcy during such shaky times.

We drive ourselves to be productive when we work from home or go through home-based learning, determined to emerge from this pandemic better, smarter, faster, fitter. Online courses. Exercise. Baking. Gardening. Comfort food. Anything to stem the fear, anxiety, isolation and disconnect from others.

I am a person who lives with depression and anxiety. For a period, I was homebound because of crippling anxiety and the sheer weight of depression. The Internet became my only window to the outside world.

Covid-19 has made me relive those years.

I remember feeling as if danger lurked everywhere, that the "outside" was unsafe and suffocating. So I isolated myself because I was already feeling disconnected from everyone else. At the same time, I constantly battled a sense of being unable to catch up with society and questioned my worth. So I did whatever I could to present that semblance of normalcy to people I knew.

I was lying to myself.

Difficult journey

After graduating in 2006, I struggled with transitioning from student to working adult.

Despite my honours degree in management with a focus on human resource and social psychology, I was unprepared for the stark transition from school to work in the banking industry. Staying in office until 9pm became the norm. I dreaded each day and braced myself for verbal abuse and petty politics.

My body began breaking down. I saw the GP every other week for gastric issues or colds. My throat was so raw from coughing that each breath would send me into a coughing fit.

I had nightmares and grew increasingly anxious at the thought of going to work. It came to a point when I could no longer control my tears. I remember sitting at the bus stop, crying and feeling embarrassed and ashamed. Here I was, a fresh graduate in her brand new G2000 blouse, matching skirt and heels, crying uncontrollably in public.

Instead of going to work that day, I visited the GP. That was when the doctor tentatively asked if there was a history of mental illness in my family.

Yes, I replied, softly.

Two weeks before my 24th birthday, four months after starting work, I was diagnosed with Major Depressive Disorder and Generalised Anxiety Disorder.

I quit my job a month later. I had lost 10kg by then.

My personal life was tumultuous as well. Before I quit my job, my boyfriend proposed. This joy was short-lived because my parents divorced soon after.

Friends noticed the physical change in me. I laughed away my sudden weight loss, saying that it was for our wedding the next year and I wanted to fit into the dress. After all, losing weight for a happy occasion seemed more socially acceptable.

Beneath the laughter, however, I was in fear – would my marriage fail? Would my future in-laws accept someone jobless and with a mental health diagnosis?

—

> Am I broken? Did I not try hard enough?
> Am I weak, a disappointment and a failure?

—

The thoughts kept swirling in my head. I withdrew from people because it became too hard to pretend all was well.

It was a perfect storm of personal and professional chaos. I was unable to find my footing. I became unmoored in my sense of self and sank fast despite my best efforts to stay afloat.

I went to a psychiatrist for the first time. I was determined to get "fixed". It turned out to be a dehumanising experience; something that made me swear off medication until much later on.

For the next four years, I went on a desperate quest for self discovery. I sought out counselling, self-help books, eastern and western medical supplements, exercise, diets. I even returned to school and earned a graduate diploma in psychology.

It didn't help.

By 2011, the depression and anxiety had worsened to a point that I was contemplating ending it all. Perhaps it was divine intervention that saved me. I told myself that I would give medication one last try. This second psychiatrist was experienced and took efforts to explain how medication would help me. For the first time, I felt like a person, not a case or a statistic.

This marked the beginning of my long, winding journey to recovery.

I took my medication faithfully, kept my appointments and communicated openly with my doctor about the side effects. I read all I could about depression and anxiety. I started seeing a therapist. She has been crucial to my survival, even till today.

My husband never gave up on me. I'd share with him how my therapy sessions went and we worked out how to manage situations and identify my triggers. He taught me what it means to truly love someone, in sickness and in health.

Empowering youths at the National University of Singapore. *Credit: Nicole K.*

Delivering a talk to students at the Institute of Mental Health. *Credit: Nicole K.*

In those times of turmoil I found solace in words. Journalling, in particular, was something I turned to during those painful times.

I found strength to get back into society. In 2012, I decided to volunteer as a therapy dog handler. That was when I stumbled into the world of publishing and landed my first writing gig with an international newspaper. Thus, I embarked on my freelance writing adventure and wrote for SMEs, MNCs and local media.

But I wanted to do more with my writing.

I believed that God could turn my mess into my life's message. I wanted to turn pain into purpose, to shortcut that process of getting help, to allow other people who struggled like me to be "seen".

So in 2014, I took a leap of faith and founded The Tapestry Project SG, a ground-up initiative that champions mental wellness and recovery through sharing first-person narratives of struggles and redemption. There you can find more stories of hope and courage.

Social researcher and author Brené Brown wrote that "owning our story and loving ourselves through that process is the bravest thing that we will ever do".

I believe that by sharing our stories of vulnerability, we break away from stigmatizing shame and isolation. My goal is to reach someone who was like me, homebound and frustrated. I want to increase access to relatable mental health information and bring together organisations that provide help and the people who need help.

I remember opening up to people about my mental health struggles. One of the first things that people told me was to "do stuff" to cure my troubles: Eat right, sleep well, get enough exercise, pursue some hobbies, look on the bright side.

These responses, to me, parallels our response to Covid-19. Although well-meaning, such "fixes" need to be balanced with vulnerability. Vulnerability is not weakness. On the contrary, the ability to talk about our struggles shows strength and courage.

When we acknowledge our shaken sense of self, our difficulties in adjusting to these sudden changes in work, priorities and relationships, we are building resilience, empathy and kindness. Through this process, we begin to look after our physical and mental health as well as others.

Recovery is not a linear process. It's a constant battle to find balance and regain your footing during times of turmoil.

During his speech on the Fortitude Budget on May 26, 2020, Deputy Prime Minister Heng Swee Keat described "fortitude" as "courage in adversity". Indeed, we need courage more than ever. We may slip and fumble during these times of instability, but let us hold fast to hope and know that our stories of vulnerability are stories of victory in the making.

Toxic masculinity needs to stop, and it starts with us

Being open with emotions should never be taboo. Sharing feelings not only helps us process them better, but it also forms stronger bonds.

by Ryan Teo

There has been much talk about gender equality in Singapore.

It's 2020 but there is still a pervasive cultural gender norm where the husband is out working to provide for the household while the wife is at home taking care of the family.

Recently, the conversation has shifted to women's rights in Singapore and the government is planning a series of reviews to address these issues.

The White Paper, entitled "Conversations on Women Development" will be an important milestone in charting the course of gender equality in Singapore for years to come.

But before we get there, there is another issue closely related to gender roles that have been affecting men – not just in Singapore but in many parts of the world as well.

Toxic masculinity perpetuates the stereotype that there is only one "acceptable" way of being a man, and that is to be stoic, strong and domineering. Anything less than being the "alpha" is a shortcoming and a "real man" must strive to attain that lofty level before he can claim to be a success.

That toxicity breeds unhealthy competition – even contempt – and when boys are brought up in that environment, it creates a problem. In 2017, a survey by the gender equality advocacy group AWARE and Ngee Ann Polytechnic found that nine in ten teenage males face pressure from society to be "manly". This pressure includes being subjected to harassment, bullying as well as physical and mental violence, among other things.

This gives you an insight into the kind of environment young men have to traverse today. This environment gives them two choices: Either conform to a particular standard of "being a man", or be ridiculed, ostracised and even hurt for being different.

Shamed into silence

"Come on bro, you're a guy. Cry for what?"

Those were the words I heard as I sat in my secondary school classroom, tears running down my face.

At the time, I was frustrated at myself for not being able to perform as well as some of my peers. They were getting good grades, making loads of friends and generally fitting in.

I was not. My inability to achieve what they could made me feel less of a person. And I was dealing with it the way I knew how: By allowing my hurt and anger at myself flow to the surface.

I remember hearing a hint of mockery in the words coming from my classmate. I didn't know why he was saying what he was saying. Perhaps he didn't know what to do with a crying classmate. Maybe he was trying to be reassuring but it came out wrong.

Whatever it is, his words didn't make me feel any better. In fact, I felt even more sub-par than I already did. However, it did make me stop crying – out of shame. My classmate's scoff shamed me and I instantly pretended as if nothing happened.

Finding a solution

Unfortunately, toxic masculinity has played a significant role in my upbringing. For years, I have been socialised to believe that to be a man, I have to be strong at all times and not show any vulnerability in any situation. Doing otherwise would make me "not a real man" but just an "attention-seeker".

Unbeknownst to everyone, I was struggling internally.

This caused me to bottle up all my negative thoughts. Whenever something upset me, I would pretend to be nonchalant and downplay it. "It's not a big deal" became my pet phrase.

That unhealthy practice only aggravated my already low self-esteem. The negativity festered and my mental health suffered.

Unbeknownst to everyone, I was struggling internally.
Credit: Unsplash / Nik Shuliahin.

I didn't even dare to let it out in private because I believed that vocalising my fears was a validation of my weaknesses.

And when those emotions eventually spilled out, I started to believe that I was too weak to be a "real man".

I gradually broke out of that spiral, thanks to a spiritual experience and after finding help from online articles. I realised that being devoid of negative emotions doesn't make me a man. It just makes me a robot.

But I want to be clear too. This is a personal journey. Let's not judge others on what we see on the surface. Just because someone doesn't show emotion, it doesn't mean that he (or she, for that matter) is incapable of experiencing emotion.

It is about finding your own truth. Get real. That's the key. What is real for you? There's nothing wrong about being the strong, silent, stoic type … if that is what you are. I am not, but I was shamed into thinking that that was the only proper way a "real man" should behave.

I believe the solution to toxic masculinity is to find who you are and to be that person. If you express yourself through sharing emotions and shedding tears, sure, go for it. But if you're the strong, silent type, it doesn't necessarily mean that you're repressing your feelings and being a slave to societal norms.

Toxic masculinity affects more people than you'd expect

After escaping my vicious cycle, I began to see how toxic masculinity still affected those around me. From among my own friends to overhearing conversations of passing strangers, I continued to notice those ever-familiar mocking statements when anyone tried to talk about their feelings.

Whenever possible, I attempted to encourage my friends to be open and allow someone to feel safe to speak when he started to share something personal. But most of the time, they would ignore me and that friend's moment of vulnerability gets met with sniggers and raised eyebrows.

Often, I could see that person flip a mental switch and sweep his thoughts under the metaphorical carpet; oh how reminiscent of how I used to respond!

This always left a lasting impression on me. Even though the person seemed okay on the outside, I knew that we couldn't see how it was still damaging him inside.

Recently, I came across an article about a group of young men in Ireland who set up a help group called the Dublin Boys Club. Before Covid, they would meet once a month to practise "real talk" – that is, to openly discuss their fears and concerns with one another – without hiding behind banter or having alcohol as a crutch to the conversation.

Even during their lockdown, they would meet virtually to talk about their worries. The members also had a WhatsApp group to share self-help materials, talk about their problems or arrange online and offline meetings.

This support group is all about supporting one another as men and ridding themselves of the idea that being vulnerable isn't manly. As one of the participants said rather colourfully, it takes great courage (he didn't use that word) to be open with a group of 20 other men.

Toxic masculinity during Covid

Reading about these Irishmen in Dublin gives me hope for what we are going through now.

We are facing a pandemic that has changed the way our lives work, some more drastically than others. Some of us have lost our jobs or loved ones. Others are lonely or angry. We are restricted in many ways and adapting to this new normal can be very stressful and harmful to our mental health.

Credit: Unsplash / Freddie Marriage.

Toxic masculinity removes our ability to cope with these new stressors. Pride and ego make us pretend to be okay even when we are not. But when it becomes too much – and it probably will – we crumble and break down.

This problem has been prominent even well before Covid. According to Samaritans of Singapore, out of the 400 suicides reported in 2019, more than two out of every three of them were men.

Reclaiming what "being a man" means

One common phrase flung at men who talk about their feelings is to "man up" or "be a man". This has perpetuated toxic stereotypes for too long. But let's not refute this phrase; let's reclaim it instead.

I would argue that telling someone to man up is totally acceptable. What needs to change is our definition of what "manning up" entails. We need to get rid of the outdated concept of the alpha male, grinding his teeth, silent in the face of pressure, or worse, over-compensating when called out, flexing his muscles, metaphorical or otherwise, to try to bluster his way out of trouble.

Imagine how it would feel like if we redefine "manning up" as "staying true to your strengths"?

We don't need to punch a bully to take him down; we can stand over the fallen and protect the bullied. We don't need to shout to be heard; we speak quietly but authoritatively for the voiceless. We don't need to be brash to be strong; we show our composure by using our hearts and minds, not just our muscles.

There is more than one way to "be a man".

A few years ago, there was a PR campaign that called into question some long-held stereotypes. Called "Like a Girl", it called out some parts of society (even women too!) for viewing doing something 'like a girl' as an insult.

Thanks to the campaign, more men (and women) are turning the meaning of the phrase around and now it is a message of empowerment. Many now view the phrase in a positive light, and they are more confident in doing what they want to do without society trying to hold them back.

What if we could run a similar campaign but call it "Being a Man"? What responses do you think we would get?

Men need to talk now, more than ever, as it will allow us to better process what we are going through. It takes a load off our chests and will help us on the road to overcoming our toxicity.

Just being human

In retrospect, I wish that I knew then (when my classmate mocked me) what I know now. Granted, I was young and impressionable and he probably was the same. On the bright side, the experience has left me wiser and more mature in my beliefs. They were hard yet vital lessons that I'm glad I was able to learn.

I hope that we as men can be more accepting of sharing our feelings with others. This not only helps us conquer our not-so-

Credit: Unsplash / Sharefaith.

happy days, but it also allows us to grow closer to our family and friends to create a more wholesome society for all.

Emotions are what make us human. Showing them isn't a sign of weakness. Rather, it's a sign of our humanity. Choosing to hide our emotions only deprives us of our right to be who we are. That is why we shouldn't create an environment that pressures men to suppress them.

Anyone can yell and beat their chest and call it courage. Bombast isn't bravery. True strength comes from daring to look inside yourself and admit that you may not be okay but you'll get better.

That, to me, is a sign of a real man.

Let's flip the script when we talk about suicide

We ignore suicidal thoughts as if that would make them go away. Instead, let's learn to talk about it, without fear or judgement.

by Jamie Wong

Let's talk about the unspeakable.

We are hearing more stories of self-harm and suicide, yet we are having the wrong conversations about it. In September 2020 alone, we have had breathless accounts of celebrity suicides of actresses like Oh In-Hye, Sei Ashina or Yuko Takeuchi. Earlier this year, a migrant worker who tested positive for Covid-19 fell to his death at Khoo Teck Puat Hospital.

Often, our conversations around suicide reflect a similar macabre fascination we have about a particularly gruesome car crash. We stop and we stare, then we move off, temporarily disconcerted before resuming life as per normal.

Credit: Jamie Wong.

We need more constructive conversations on such a real problem facing our society, especially when it is increasingly affecting our young people.

Suicide has been described as an irreversible solution to an often temporary problem.

"It's not the life they want to end. It's about the suffering; they just don't want the suffering to continue," mental health advocate Jonathan Kuek tells The Pride.

When someone is suicidal, they are unable to see outside of their desperate situation. Wanting their suffering to end yet feeling trapped by circumstances, they may believe that taking their own life is the only option left.

Samaritans of Singapore's chief executive Gasper Tan explains that this tunnel vision makes suicidal individuals feel empty and alone.

"The perception that no one is around as a pillar of support can amplify the feelings of despair."

Who's affected

In theory, there are certain risk factors that can determine how likely someone would choose to end their lives. Factors ranging from social economic status to mental health conditions can indicate the likelihood of suicidal behaviour.

However, many researchers agree that it is almost impossible to tell who is truly at risk. Jonathan says: "In a real-world setting, I doubt anyone would be able to confidently say who will be most likely to attempt to end their lives via suicide."

In 2019, 400 people killed themselves in Singapore. If you think that number isn't much, try telling that to the 400 families left behind. More worryingly, the number of calls to helplines have increased. Suicide remains the leading cause of death among our youths aged 10 to 29.

Not just in Singapore, but across the world, suicide rates have increased as Covid-19 has caused people to worry about their livelihoods.

But why don't we talk?

In his advocacy, Jonathan has seen people ending their lives over tough life events such as relationship woes, work stress or money issues.

Credit: Jamie Wong.

These problems, although common, can have dire consequences if not talked about. But once these feelings are shared, he says, very often these issues can be resolved.

So why do many people choose to remain silent? Gasper tells The Pride that it boils down to fear – of judgement and of being seen as weak.

"The stigma and silence attached to suicide creates fear and inhibits people from speaking out," he says.

People sometimes label suicide as a selfish choice, but that's the wrong approach. This could contribute to the suicidal person's belief that they are a burden to those around them, which increases their fear and isolation.

In many cases, Jonathan says, suicidal people have genuinely tried to voice out their issues, but are rejected or ignored. Hence, some create a facade, pretending to be well even when they harbour suicidal thoughts. Sometimes, they even end up believing the pretence, which discourages them from seeking help early.

Turning good intentions into good actions

But Gasper believes that most of a suicidal person's loved ones have good intentions, even though their actions may not reflect that. "While the topic of suicide may cause others to be startled initially, more often than not they will still want to help," he says.

He explains that the stigma surrounding suicide can be removed only when we address it openly.

For such conversations to be normalised, Jonathan says, we need more proactive measures: Don't just list the distress signs; teach people to be better listeners.

Decriminalising attempted suicide is a good first step, as authorities can now focus on getting help to those struggling with suicidal feelings. But more needs to be done.

"We need a cultural shift," Jonathan says, referring to the need to further untangle the misconceptions surrounding suicide.

A cry for attention or a cry for help?

While suicidal feelings can be a symptom of an underlying mental health issue, it can also simply be part of a human life experience.

Let's not be too quick to conclude that all those who are suicidal have a mental health condition. To do so would be to disregard their individual struggles.

Gasper raises another common mistake about people who attempt suicide. "There is a misconception that people who talk about suicide or attempt suicide are just seeking attention and will not go through with the act," he says.

However, it should never be brushed aside.

This is because an attempt to take one's own life is usually a call for help instead of a desire for attention. Often, it is the only way they think they can express their distress after all other methods have seemed to fail. "What they need is not attention but genuine care and support," says Jonathan.

Credit: Jamie Wong.

Both Gasper and Jonathan say that it is essential that all mentions of suicide or suicide attempts should be treated seriously and not as a form of attention-seeking. If someone is threatening suicide, get help immediately.

Another common misconception about suicide is that talking about it encourages it. Jonathan elaborates on this, saying that the media may play up suicide stories, especially of celebrities, to grab more eyeballs. If it's left to stand on its own, without proper context, this sensationalism can be dangerous when someone wrongly identifies with the message.

We should talk about suicide in a safe zone, opening doors for communication between suicidal individuals and the people around them. Done right, it can be a relief for those contemplating suicide to feel safe in sharing their struggles.

Be approachable

"We need to create a psychologically safe environment, and demonstrate that there is care being shown to them on a regular basis," Jonathan explains. From his observations, most of the time, struggling individuals just need a listening ear. "Sometimes, you don't even need to provide a solution."

Jokes about suicide can be a double-edged sword. It could be a coping mechanism or a cry for help. But don't immediately jump to conclusions. "A passing joke is usually not an issue," Jonathan says. Poking fun at stressful events has proven to relax people and build rapport.

If you hear a friend joke about suicide and you feel something is off, the best thing to do is to outright ask him how serious he is. Even if he brushes it off, it can set the stage for a more genuine conversation about deeper issues in the future.

"Trust your instincts, if you notice that there may be something amiss, do reach out and check in. It is always better to make a supportive attempt than none at all," Gasper says.

Be genuine

But beware of sounding too glib or just paying lip service. Gasper says that it all boils down to body language and word choice. "Personal anecdotes and overused phrases like 'things will get better' and 'if I can do it, you can too' may seem like harmless encouragement, but they actually disregard and invalidate the feelings of the individual in crisis."

He recommends listening attentively and acknowledging the struggles they are going through. As people fear being judged, refrain from imposing your own advice or judgement. Aim to understand their struggles, and be comfortable in not providing any solutions.

If you suspect someone to be harbouring suicidal thoughts, check in with them and explain why you're worried about them. It is best to reach out to them privately, Gasper says, with a simple "how are you?" to know you care. "Your ability to notice the small details may signal to the individual that you are genuinely concerned."

Be understanding

Even those who want to talk about suicide the right way need to be wary of getting on their high horse.

"We need to stop virtue signalling on what is the right way to talk about suicide," Jonathan says. By reprimanding those who joke about suicide or brushing off those who think suicidal people are merely attention-seekers, we may end up creating a politically-correct zone of empty platitudes instead of encouraging meaningful discourse.

"This is a misguided way of talking about sensitive issues. We need to have more perspectives and not hold on to a single one."

He encourages embracing the diversity of worldviews when discussing suicide. It is important to understand those who see suicide in a different way before coming to a unifying narrative. "That's when we start to have real, uncomfortable, potentially impactful discussions around mental health and mental illness."

Be self-aware

Of course, as any long-term caregiver knows, there is a cost to providing support to others.

Jonathan highlights the importance of removing yourself from the situation from time to time to restore emotional capacity. This could come in many forms; be it surrounding yourself with friends who are in a better space in their lives or engaging in positive self-talk. Constantly reminding yourself that you are not obligated to save someone and you are simply holding a safe mental space for them to retreat to can help regulate your emotional health too.

"It's also about being very clear about your emotional and psychological boundaries," Jonathan adds.

Ultimately, providing informal caregiving and social support should be temporary. Seeking formal professional support can help with their issues from a more holistic perspective.

"And most importantly," Jonathan concludes, "if anything goes wrong, you need to know that it's not your fault and you've done all that you can. Someone you're supporting choosing to end their life, as painful as it is, is really not a commentary or indictment on you as a person or your abilities to support others."

If you are feeling distressed, or know someone who is feeling suicidal, get help immediately. Talk to somebody.

Helplines
- National Care Hotline: 1800 202 6868
- Samaritans of Singapore: 1800 221 4444
- Institute of Mental Health: 6389 2222
- Silver Ribbon Singapore: 6385 3714
- Tinkle Friends (for children): 1800 2744 788
- TOUCHline (Counselling): 1800 377 2252

It's okay not to be okay, so let's talk about it

You needn't be in dire situations to suffer the effects of stress in your life. Mental wellness is crucial for everyone in our new normal.

by Solomon Lim

Let's talk about the elephant in the room.

Sometimes, I don't know how to talk to my friends.

Some of those who know me would counter that statement with the astute observation that to have that problem, I would first need to make some friends, but that's fodder for a different column.

Back to my point. I get tongue-tied sometimes.

It's not something that's new. But something that I've noticed a lot more now. And I don't think I'm the only one.

It's almost as if the circuit breaker has flipped a switch, and we suddenly don't know how to talk to someone else in person any more. For all our Zoom meetings and Hangout chats and Teams conferences, we seem to have lost the ability to relate to someone else outside of a small webcam window.

Perhaps it's just me, or perhaps it's not. Like it or not, how we react to people who aren't in our immediate family circle has changed. If you don't have this problem, then congratulations, dear friend, the rest of this piece wouldn't really make sense to you.

For the rest of us, I've got a question... how do you handle it?

Online smiles, offline sighs

Talking to someone in person gives us visual cues to a conversation. So much of talking to a person is about body language and aural cues. There is an entire unspoken dialogue when you meet someone face to face. The slump of his shoulders, or a bounce in her step; a lilt in her voice or a grumble in his tone.

How do you try to puzzle it out through a tiny window and tinny audio?

Let me tell you how I do it.

I don't.

Now, in some of my online meetings, I plaster on a big smile and a cheery voice, on top of the collared shirt I wear over my home shorts.

I grin and I nod and I participate and I contribute. Then when the meeting ends and the video light goes off, I heave a sigh of relief and glance at my watch. Two hours to go before the next meeting. And the cycle repeats. I'm working and I'm working and things do get done, but I'm missing out on that basic human need for interaction.

When does FaceTime really mean face time?

Living in our winter of discontent

Everyone carries their own burdens in our Covid world. It may be the worries of a harried worker or the fears of a tireless frontliner. A business owner may be stressing over the red in his ledger or a cabby may be panicking over the emptiness of his back seat. And above it all, the spectre of retrenchment looms.

But even if we don't fall into any of these categories (and I'm blessed with caring colleagues and a sense of purpose in a stable job), we shouldn't be so quick to dismiss that low-key background hum of discontent as we work from home or study online.

This is the reality of the "new normal", I'm told. "Get used to it", I'm advised. Okay, noted. With thanks. But how do those statements actually help me?

And if you're anything like me, how does that help you?

> "So many of us are gliding along like swans,
> so graceful on the surface,
> but paddling furiously beneath the water."

Like a musician friend of mine who remarked that thanks to Covid and the restrictions that come with it, there is an entire cohort of young artists who are at a loss over what to do next in their chosen profession.

Dare to push the boundaries of friendship

We should talk about our lives. And properly. Don't just scratch the surface with a superficial "hi and bye". How many times have you spoken to a friend whom you suspect is hurting – emotionally or economically – and he fobs you off with an "I'm okay, I'm okay!", or an "*aiyah*, like that *lah*, can't do much about it, just endure *lor*".

We should dare to push a little more, not out of a perverse need to satisfy our curiosity, but out of a genuine concern for a friend.

True friends pay attention, not lip service.

We should also know when to talk, and sometimes simply to listen. To offer a solution or just a shoulder to lean on. But we are gradually losing that skill as we peer at the world through the monitor screen or the smartphone.

I'm not knocking virtual interactions. Given a choice between an online chat or none at all, my vote is always for the former. There is a lot of potential for technology to be a conduit for empathy. And there are many stories of how a comforting voice over the phone or a concerned face in a virtual chatroom have proved to be the difference between life and death.

My point is that it shouldn't replace what we've been doing all this time – all those non-verbal actions we do to let people know that we are okay. Of course, we need to consider safe distancing norms now. Replace that handshake at work with a namaste; that fistbump at the gym with an elbow or ankle tap; that arm around your friend with a grin that travels past your mask to your eyes.

Yes, let's adapt to the new normal, but let's not retreat from it.

Looking forward to our glorious summer

Which is why I'm glad that the government is making plans for us to move into Phase 3.

I'm also glad for events like the National Council of Social Service's Beyond The Label virtual fest on September 26 and 27, which seeks to remove the stigma from talking about mental wellness.

This year's BTL campaign focuses on Singaporeans who may be facing socio-economic uncertainties and are under mental distress.

NCSS wants to encourage people to be open to seeking and accepting help early, and to develop mental fortitude to face life's stressors and challenges. It has also launched a short film that will resonate with many Singaporeans going through tough times now.

The fest culminates with a virtual concert on September 27 at 8 pm, with performances from local artists like Stephanie Sun, Kit Chan, Tosh Zhang and Taufik Batisah, as well as musicians from the 3am Music Collective.

These performers aren't just playing to entertain. They know what it is to struggle with mental health conditions. And they are talking about it openly to signal to all of us that hey, it's okay not to be okay. So let's talk about it.

I want to be able to look past the mask (both real and virtual) on a friend's face and ask: "Hey bro, I know you say you are okay, but are you *really* okay?"

That's when the real conversation starts.

Parenting our children

"Students who are loved at home, come to school to learn. And students who aren't, come to school to be loved."

Veteran educator shares how social work and education are her guiding lights.

by Melissa Wong

She is inspired by the much-loved Japanese book *Totto-Chan: The Little Girl at the Window*.

The book celebrates an unconventional approach to education that combines learning with fun, freedom and love. And veteran educator Soh Beng Mui believes that is the path to bring up children as responsible citizens.

She recalls her first home visit vividly. It was to a student's house on Pipit Road.

She tells The Pride: "I'd never seen a place like that. What caught my attention were the groups of people with children in prams and smokers congregating at the void deck. It got me thinking – what was going to happen to the children?"

At the time, Beng Mui was vice-principal of NorthLight School, a specialised school for less academically inclined students. She explains that the students simply have a different worldview.

She says: "It's no use telling them that what we want them to do is good for them, because at that age they're not mature enough to understand. What they see as the norm is that nobody works in the household – people are in and out of rehab centres, parents are incarcerated, and some of them have unwilling caregivers."

Today, the 48-year-old principal of Juying Secondary School in Jurong West has more than 24 years of experience under her belt but still fondly remembers her two years as vice-principal at NorthLight as one of her best. Her role there married her two callings – education and social work – and she gleaned a lot from the people she met.

During those two years, she made regular visits to hospitals and even the Institute of Mental Health (IMH), because her students were often the victims of abuse, violence or neglect.

Beng Mui says: "It toughened me immensely, but it was so meaningful because it wasn't just education we were talking about. The challenge came from finding out how we were going to make the students see the importance of school. For many of them, being educated is not a priority. They are easy targets for the bad guys out there – as runners for loan sharks or to sell illegal DVDs [back then] in Geylang."

While she and the teachers at NorthLight couldn't help every single student, Beng Mui believes in planting the seeds in each child, hoping that down the road, there would be others to carry on the work they have started.

Strong support structure

Now, at Juying Secondary School, she emphasises building a strong support structure in school to accompany what is taught at home.

"I tell my teachers that we are privileged to have close contact with our children, something we should leverage," says Beng Mui, who works closely with her student development and special-education needs teams.

Beng Mui (second from left) with students from NorthLight School. *Credit: Soh Beng Mui.*

A school walkabout is the most crucial part of her everyday routine, especially since she believes in getting to know every child personally. In fact, her goal is to get to know three new children in school every day.

She also conducts Character and Citizenship Education lessons. So it is no surprise that Beng Mui has built a good rapport with the majority of her thousand-plus students.

"I make it clear to my staff that this is the standard of relationship I expect, especially from form teachers," she says.

She even set her teachers a challenge: To be able to recognise their students outside school, when they are in home attire, a goal that she says with a smile they are still working on.

The path hasn't always been been easy. There were a few episodes where she had discovered that some children were having problems at home, which had gone unnoticed by their teachers. These problems manifested physically in dirty uniforms or tattered shoes.

Building gratitude into the school culture

"The biggest thing I have done since taking over the school is culture-building because I really see the potential in both students and staff," she shares. "The school's results are at a satisfactory level. As long as I do not compromise on that, the teachers are quite happy to come on board with me on the things I want to do."

Last year, she introduced a passion module that allows students across all streams to study topics like art, sports and nature, amongst others.

Explains Beng Mui: "I believe in taking the students out of the school into the community for projects, learning journeys and advocacy work."

In 2019, she launched a gratitude module and revamped the prefectorial board into a student council. Every year, she also encourages the graduating cohort to come up with a legacy project. Last year's graduating students came up with an idea based on Singapore Kindness Movement's mascot called "The Singa in Me" – a project that impressed her.

The project, launched this year, inspired a gratitude corner and raised funds for school janitors and families of financially challenged students. The money was raised from selling cards, which were

Parenting our children 89

One of the programmes Beng Mui started to inspire gratitide at Juying Secondary School is The Singa in Me. *Credit: Soh Beng Mui.*

The gratitude wall at Juying Secondary School. *Credit: Facebook / Juying Secondary School.*

placed at the gratitude wall, as well as donations from staff.

This is part of the trust within the positive school culture that Beng Mui is building. The trust within the staff ensures that they are ready to help whenever asked. And they did, many donating all or part of the money that they got from this year's Solidarity Budget.

She says: "The school raised $14,500 from the staff alone and it left me in tears. I was only expecting around $5,000, which is already a great amount. So, we managed to help 29 families staying in rental and one-room flats and parents who have lost their jobs during this period.

"When we gave them the money, it was amazing to see the smiles on their faces. It was such a beautiful thing that happened during the pandemic period."

Credit: Facebook / Juying Secondary School.

Multiple pathways to success

In Singapore, Beng Mui says, the education system pumps in resources to help underperforming students – something not every country does.

"To put it bluntly, they were once perceived as liabilities in society, but we stay true to our mission that no child should be left behind. Because we truly believe that every child is unique and every child can learn and succeed. From that perspective, I am very thankful for our system," she says.

Nevertheless, there is room for improvement, especially in the paperchase – we shouldn't just talk about change, we should act on it.

"When it comes to the race [for grades], it's a societal thing. The enlightenment of stakeholders is crucial. If you truly believe in building an inclusive society then stay true to it, not just agree to it on paper. I've seen people agree that getting a degree isn't necessary, but yet their own children ought to. As long as we hold on to that mindset, we will never be able to fully appreciate the pathways that are readily available. "

So what does a positive school culture look like?

"For students, it's about discipline, having school pride, and being gracious," Beng Mui says. "These are the three key things that I set up for the kids. And I told my staff that it will not be different for them. What I want to see in the kids, I must also see in the staff – it's a simple correlation."

In the same way, she also goes out of her way to build relationships with her staff one-to-one.

"Because I know enough of their work, I want to know them as a person, and I want them to know me too… I am very appreciative of my teachers. They invest so much of themselves into the lives of their students, aside from their own heavy commitments at home."

A system built on love

This is where Beng Mui brings up the school based on *Totto-chan*, the semi-autobiographical book of UNICEF Goodwill Ambassador Tetsuko Kuroyanagi, who wrote about her childhood experiences at Tomoe Gakuen, a Tokyo elementary school during World War II.

Says Beng Mui: "It goes back to understanding the child from the onset. Problems always manifest in behaviour and people pick it out as a behavioural issue… But it is when we really talk to them that we can make a difference in their lives.

"This is something I tell my teachers – try to see things from their worldview first, don't be so anxious to show your worldview. They've got so many people telling them they're wrong, it doesn't help to just be a part of that number."

One quote from American educator Nicholas Ferroni sums up her beliefs: "Students who are loved at home, come to school to learn. And students who aren't, come to school to be loved."

Beng Mui says: "It's very powerful and I'm always repeating this. We have many kids who are not being loved at home. Even if they have an intact and fully functional family, the kind of attention and love they need may not be there. There are so many kids whose lives we can touch."

Students are taught to be disciplined, to have school pride and to be gracious.
Credit: Facebook / Juying Secondary School.

A couple's kind act helps Primary 6 pupil reach school in time for PSLE exam

When a girl asked if she could borrow a phone, a couple instead went the extra mile and called a ride to get her to school.

by Ryan Teo

The biggest nightmare a student can face is being late for an exam.

Worse if it is a national exam, like the PSLE.

That was exactly what happened to one 12-year-old girl when she realised that she could not make it to school in time for her Mathematics paper.

Thankfully, a kind stranger came to her rescue.

On Friday, Oct 2, 2020, Jacinta Oriole Putri approached a couple to ask if they could help call her parents as she didn't have a phone. The woman, Shradha Iyer, saw her distress and asked her what was wrong.

Shradha tells The Pride: "We were going for a morning walk when a little girl approached us to ask if we could call her parents. When I asked her if she was feeling unwell, she said no, she is running late for her exam and the bus had not arrived. We tried to call her parents but they didn't pick up, so we asked which school she goes to and what bus she was taking."

Shradha and her husband Shreedhar.
Credit: Shradha Iyer.

Despite only meeting Jacinta for the first time, Shradha, 45, who works as a regional product manager at fragrance company Givaudan Singapore, spared no effort in helping the girl get to her school.

"It was already 7am and she told us that her exam was at 7.30am and the bus ride would take 45 minutes. So we knew that she would not make it in time for the exam. That's why we decided to book a ride for her," explains Shradha.

She even went the extra mile to call the Grab driver after the journey to ensure that Jacinta reached her school safely. Afterwards, Shradha's husband Shreedhar messaged Jacinta's father to tell him what had happened.

Thanks to this kind gesture, Jacinta was able to make it to school on time for her PSLE exam.

A father's gratitude

Jacinta's father, Deni Suryadi, 41, who works as an engineer, was so moved by Shradha and Shreedhar's kind act that he posted a tribute video on his Instagram page to thank them.

It was a series of unfortunate events that caused his daughter to be late on Friday, he tells The Pride.

Deni, who has three other children, explains: "My daughter actually planned to go to school with her friends. Unfortunately, they were unable to turn up at the bus stop due to a miscommunication. So my daughter waited for a long time at the bus stop without realising that she was already late."

It was only after she realised what time it was that Jacinta approached Shradha and Shreedhar to ask for help in calling her father.

And the couple's kindness didn't stop there, says Deni. When he tried to pay for the ride, Shreedhar politely declined and told him that they were just glad that Jacinta could make it to school on time.

Putting herself in others' shoes

For Shradha, her act of kindness came naturally because she could understand the anxiety Jacinta was going through.

Shradha says: "I am a mother who is always stressed about her children going for their exams as they go to school in Bedok and we live in Bukit Batok. So I could relate to how Jacinta was feeling especially because it was the PSLE and she was very stressed. I

Deni with his wife and children. Jacinta is third from left, wearing spectacles.
Credit: Deni Suryadi.

wouldn't want my child to be in her shoes so I wanted to do my best to help."

Deni is immensely grateful for the extraordinary gesture the couple extended to his daughter.

He says: "Hopefully this kindness will be an example to everyone to help people in need regardless of race, religion and nationality."

Shradha also hopes that people in society would be more understanding to others.

She says: "This is what we all need to do in this world, to be kind to one another… and have empathy without any expectations. It's something normal that everyone should think of doing."

Do our grades define us? Learning more about ourselves from our O-Level results

Getting exam results is nerve-wrecking but keep a positive perspective, no matter the outcome.

by Jamie Wong

O-Level results are around the corner.

What better way to kick off 2021 with D-Day in the middle of a pandemic?

Even in times like these, some O-Level traditions still stand. The Bell Curve God is still around to bless us. We take solace in following exam meme accounts. We calculate how many marks we've lost based on answer sheets from tuition centres, and receive cheery poly and private school open house flyers in the mail.

Our decade-long school journey is coming to an end, and every decision you were "supposed" to make is rushing at you all at once.

We're all trying to reassure each other, but both you and I know that being kind to yourself when you don't get the grades you're hoping for is easier said than done. We all have expectations, be it from ourselves, our teachers or parents.

In fact, the suspense is more nail-biting than the actual results. The grades themselves are unpredictable. Some students leave blanks and skip questions, yet do well. Others slog away for a paper but do not perform up to expectations.

I'm sure you've heard something along the lines of "your grades don't define you, don't be too hard on yourself", and brushed it off as well-meaning but unempathetic advice.

Well, I'm someone whose teachers called a student with "wasted" potential. I was "smart, but in the wrong areas", they said.

Fair point – who else would painstakingly draw elaborate physics puns at the back of the exam paper instead of checking through for potential mistakes? (I passed, much to my teacher's surprise.) Similarly, I enjoyed my time exercising my vocabulary in debate club, but my English grades never reflected it.

> I never passed analysing ads in graphic stimulus
> nor caught all the points in summary writing;
> I could never draw a straight grid in art. But today,
> I'm in marketing, I'm a writer and I'm an artist.

Our competitive education system may lead us to believe that if we don't make the cut for a subject at school, we would keep failing at it for the rest of our lives. And should you fall, it would be hard to get a second chance – there are several hurdles for those who wish to retake subjects. It's like Russian roulette – one stroke of bad luck and you're done.

Our academic culture also normalises critiquing our performance, no matter how good it is. You did good? You could have done better. You did really well? Maybe you don't deserve full credit for it.

To teens, these are the first major stressors they encounter, and it can manifest in extreme ways.

Focus on outcomes, not on grades

I'm not saying we shouldn't take responsibility for the results we get just because it is stressful. After all, life is about dealing with such pressures and some healthy competition is good.

It is the over-emphasis on grades, specifically top scores, that can lead to toxic behaviour.

The fact is, your grades do define you. Not acknowledging that is to ignore the reasons for assessment and examination.

What most people are really trying to do when they say that "grades don't define you", is to reassure you not to feel bad if you miss the mark.

But missing the mark isn't necessarily a bad thing.

Success and failure both help you gauge your strengths and weaknesses – the key is perspective.

If you failed math, you could either question your intelligence or decide that numbers aren't exactly your thing. If you flopped humanities or failed a language, you could either decide that you're incompetent or that memorising keywords and fancy phrases just isn't your strong suit.

You are responsible for deciding how your grades reflect you. You have the power to decide what you can learn about yourself from this exam.

We often forget a syllabus is really just a list of curated information of what we "should" comprehend at any particular educational level.

And since we'll probably never have to directly apply most of whatever we have learnt to the real world, why not focus on what the process of studying those subjects has taught us instead?

For example, drawing a graph to find out the price of a pen teaches us to spot patterns in chaos. Answering an essay question on the Cuban Missile Crisis teaches us how to organise our thoughts and argue a case.

You can also love a subject without having to get a good grade. History is more than World War II. Chemistry is more than dipping metals in acid and Physics isn't just swinging a pendulum. How tailored can a global syllabus be to your individual interests and abilities? Develop your personal calling instead.

Remember to be kind to yourself by being truthful to yourself. Reflect on your strengths and weaknesses based on the skills you've developed from studying the subject, instead of fixating on scores and results.

Look forward, but take off those rose-tinted glasses

After the O-Levels, there are so many paths to choose and options to weigh. This transition period will kick up a whirlwind of emotions.

If you get your desired tertiary education course or are given more options to choose from, congratulations! But beware of tunnel vision.

There are always going to be surprises around the corner; you might not end up where you want to be, or you make it, only to realise that it's not your cup of tea.

It's important to manage your expectations and acknowledge emotionally difficult situations – beyond just getting the results.

A friend of mine really wanted to study animation as she had been lauded for her talent in art. But when the semester started, what she thought would be a cakewalk turned out tougher than expected. She wasn't mentally prepared, and had to take a break.

For people like my friend, or those who end up somewhere they don't really want to be, it's not the end of the world. Approach everything with an open mind – after all, going to school is just one of the many ways to obtain knowledge.

It's okay if you choose to switch routes halfway, even if others may frown at you for not sticking to your decision. Personally, I think it's braver to give up painstaking progress to start afresh at what you really want to do.

Also remember that unpredictability doesn't end after the O-Levels. I know people who dropped out of junior college for polytechnic studies. Some leave integrated studies to pursue their passions. I know friends who've left STEM courses to study art and design, or those with a knack in IT finding a bigger love for the humanities.

Whether you can get into your dream course or not, remember that there are always tough choices to make, just as there will be doors opened for you.

So as you prepare yourself for an uncertain future, don't forget to prepare yourself emotionally, too.

Take time to reflect where you are in life and have honest conversations with trusted ones. Find a deeper, positive side to your results, but also manage your expectations.

Most importantly, remember that life goes beyond the paper chase. Wait until the dust settles and your emotions – high or low – recover before making a major decision.

And take heart: Regardless of your results – good or bad – you'll live and you'll learn!

How do you talk to your child about their grades?

Results are not as important as helping our children find the support and encouragement that they need.

by Solomon Lim

It's the last week of school. And what a year it has been!

The December holidays are around the corner and most parents I know are either breathing a sigh of relief that this Covid-disrupted school year is finally coming to an end, or are stressing out over how to keep the kids entertained for the full six weeks without a short holiday to break the monotony – or both.

Mostly both.

But before we get to that finish line, there's that last hurdle to cross. (In fact, it's still not the end yet for the A-level students… hang in there, guys!) That's the progress reports aka "the moment where you decide if it's time to send your kid for more tuition".

To be fair, by now, most of our children's results would already be known and most of us parents would have already had that dreaded chat with their teachers. Well, at least this year, we could do that troublesome parent-teacher meeting online (I'm ashamed to say that I missed mine because another virtual meeting overran, ahem).

For sandwich generation-ers like myself, having to worry about my kid's results is yet another bad-tasting cherry on top of a very sour sundae that is 2020.

Thankfully, she's doing okay at school so I can happily go back to stressing about the economy.

But there's one last thing I haven't done yet. Something which I daresay some of us tend to forget in our busy-ness of trying to get everything in order for our kids.

We are so focused on talking to the teachers, to our spouse, to our fellow parents, comparing results and tsk-ing over that *kiasu* auntie or wah-ing over that oh-so-clever friend of your kid's (every class has one), that we often forget the most important task.

That is, to talk to our children about how they feel about their results.

Not talk at them, mind you. Talk to them. Ask them if they are happy with how they did or sad over something they didn't do.

Then stop and listen.

It is important that we do this, because it gives them a chance to share their hopes and fears with us.

Judging from the number of rants on online forums like Reddit, young Singaporeans do feel the stress of the exams. Would you rather them venting to total strangers (albeit sometimes with positive responses) or complaining to you, where you can do something about it?

Different children, different definitions of success

A good friend of mine and a fellow parent was confiding in me recently about the challenges that he faces. His older daughter is musically inclined but faces some difficulties in school.

My friend, a private-hire driver, has had a lean year and is torn over what to do. His finances are limited and he needs to provide for his wife and two daughters, not just the older one. And music lessons are expensive.

When I asked him about his plans, he just shook his head and sighed. "I want to give her the best but I don't know how to balance. Times are bad now. *Aiyah*, just do my best *lor*, what to do?"

Another friend was recounting how his two kids have rather drastic differences in expectations for their results and that's alright with him. "My daughter gets grumpy if she doesn't score above 90 in her subjects... my son however, when he got above 50 in his mother tongue, the whole family went out for a celebration!"

"We need to celebrate the little milestones. And we never compare him with his sister. His sister also helps him in his work, in between their love-hate relationship!"

These anecdotes illustrate how different our children are. And how important it is for us as parents to celebrate those differences.

Despite our best efforts, our society still tends to limit success, at least at primary and secondary school levels, to a narrow definition.

That's why I am so inspired by educators who want to change this definition.

It reminded me of a popular quote widely attributed to Albert Einstein: "Everyone is a genius. But if you judge a fish by its ability to climb a tree, it will live its whole life believing that it is stupid."

Teach outside the box

I recently read Helen E. Buckley's short story, "The Little Boy". It's a wonderfully poignant tale of a child who just wants to learn. You can google it, but to summarise, it goes something like this:

> *A boy went to school and one day, the teacher said: "Today we are going to make a picture."*
> *"Good!" thought the little boy. He liked to make pictures.*
> *He could make all kinds: Lions and tigers, chickens and cows, trains and boats.*
> *And he took out his box of crayons and began to draw.*
> *But the teacher said: "Wait! It is not time to begin!"*
> *And she waited until everyone looked ready.*
> *"Now," said the teacher, "we are going to make flowers."*
> *"Good!" thought the little boy. He liked to make flowers.*
> *And he began to make beautiful ones with his pink and orange and blue crayons.*
> *But the teacher said: "Wait! And I will show you how."*
> *And she drew a flower on the blackboard.*
> *It was red, with a green stem. "There," said the teacher. "Now you may begin."*

The story goes on to describe how, through rote teaching without individual attention, a naturally curious and exuberant boy gets his excitement for learning curtailed to an almost robot-like level. The story ends with the boy moving to a new school, and having another teacher ask him to draw a picture.

> *When she came to the little boy, she said: "Don't you want to make a picture?"*

> "Yes," said the little boy. "What are we going to make?"
> "I don't know until you make it," said the teacher.
> "How shall I make it?" asked the little boy.
> "Why, any way you like," said the teacher.
> "And any colour?" asked the little boy.
> "Any colour," said the teacher. "If everyone made the same picture and used the same colours, how would I know who made what, and which was which?"
> "I don't know," said the little boy. And he began to draw a flower. It was red, with a green stem.

—

Some have taken this story as a criticism of rote-based teaching and a one-size-fits-all approach. I agree. But instead of blaming schools and education systems, we should take a positive approach.

Educating an entire cohort of children requires a balancing act of time, resources and commitment. And teachers, wonderful as they are, should not be held responsible for the entirety of our children's education. Neither can education systems, as comprehensive as they can be, totally cater to our children's individual needs.

That's why parents are so important in this equation. What our children learn in school, we must follow up at home.

Which is why I appreciate so much my private-driver friend's commitment to giving the best he can to his daughter, even though she isn't scoring as well as her friends in the classroom.

And why I also appreciate parents who don't compare their children with other people's kids or, heaven forbid, incite sibling rivalry between theirs.

We need to sit down with our kids and say, to effect, "Wait! How do you feel about your results?" or, especially for the older ones, who may chafe at too much parental control, "Is there anything I can do to help you?".

Encourage them to know that they are individuals in their abilities, interests and motivation. There may be a "one-size-fits-all" approach in the classroom, but there should be a "you-are-my-unique-child" mentality back home.

This may sound counter-intuitive but hear me out when I say this: Results are secondary. Character is what is important. Your child may not have found their niche in life. They may struggle with Physics or Chemistry, Geography or History; they may not qualify for an "elite" school or a six-year programme. But that's just one possible avenue of success. If your child has found their path, wonderful! If not, even better – their calling is yet to be discovered.

If they are still searching for their way in life, don't be too quick to dampen their spirits by labelling them as "difficult" or "failures". Don't be too fast to streamline and stereotype them into "science-y", "arts-y", or dare I say it, "farts-y" #dadjokes.

That's what I do with my girl. In fact, I often say to her: "I'm not so concerned about your results so long as I know you have tried your best. You will find what you're good at. And when you do, lean into it. Scoring is secondary. Finding what makes you interested and engaged is when you learn to fly."

Now, if you don't mind me, I've got to google for ways of how to spend the holidays working from home with a boisterous 10-year-old without involving copious amounts of screentime.

OKLETSGO made me pen a letter to my daughters

When the hosts of a popular podcast drew flak for their casual misogyny, a mother decided to teach her daughter about sexism.

by Mirta Syazanna

It took President Halimah Yacob, the Mufti of Singapore and a number of women to voice their concerns before a trio of ex-DJs from OKLETSGO – Dzar Ismail, 34, Dyn Norahim, 38, and Raja Razie, 38 – finally made their apology on Monday.

Over the last week (June 2020), women across the country had spoken up about the lewd and disrespectful way the hosts speak about women on the show, which calls itself the number one podcast in Singapore. With over 250 episodes published, each with more than 100,000 listeners per episode, OKLETSGO's content is often subtly peppered with crude remarks over women's bodies and sexual innuendos.

Instead of acknowledging the legitimate concerns, the ex-radio DJs chose to favour ratings over taking responsibility for their actions. Before President Halimah's reprimand on June 15, the trio had published a non-apology and a 10-minute podcast where they claimed they were being attacked because of their wide reach. They constantly trumpet their "no-holds-barred" style and an oft-used defence of "if you don't like what we say, don't listen".

Unfortunately, turning the dial doesn't turn off the misogyny. It's the aural equivalent of sticking your fingers in your ears to drown out unhealthy noise. It doesn't stop others from hearing it.

Let's be clear. Nobody has asked them to shut down their platform. In fact, it is progressive that the top Singaporean podcast is helmed by a group of minorities. However, it is unfortunate that the group seems to normalise certain types of behaviour that shouldn't be acceptable in this day and age. And they are doing it on a public platform.

Which is why I am so grateful to find that concerned Singaporeans have spoken up. And if Dzar Ismail, Dyn Norahim and Raja Razie are committed to trying to "push the boundaries" as they say they are, then they must acknowledge and respect it when these boundaries push back.

If these men still don't see the problems of misogyny and male chauvinism in a world after the #MeToo and #TimesUp movements, I am left to think about how my two young daughters may grow up in a society that breeds this sexist culture, and in the words of Taylor Swift – wondering if they'd get there (to the top) quicker if they were men.

This saga will pass, and hopefully the men of OKLETSGO would take a genuine look and reassessment of their platform. They have an opportunity to speak to many and they have shown in the past to be able to do meaningful and thoughtful non-mainstream content without having to descend into crudity and superficiality. Talking about taboo topics is good, using these topics like a punchline or using guests as a prop for cheap jokes and casual misogyny is not.

My four- and five-year-old may be too young to understand the discrimination me and fellow women in my generation may experience from time to time, but I hope when they are older, they can find strength in this letter whenever they need it:

Dear Daughters,
I don't know what the future holds, but I promise to raise you to be a person of character. I promise to teach you to make your own decisions and defend not only your rights, but also the rights of others. There will be moments of self-doubt and challenges to overcome, but remember these words that can make you a stronger and better individual.

Be your own person

> "Do you want to meet the love of your life?
> Look in the mirror."
> **– Byron Katie**

No one owns you. Anybody that calls you "mine" in a way other than which is romantic, is lying. Your body is yours, your mind is yours, your soul is yours – use it well. Value your independence because it allows you to do more than what society thinks you can – women are not only meant to stay home and raise a family. Plenty of women have proven to be able to run a company at the same time. Be self-sufficient, so that your fate will not be in the hands of those who want to control you. Invest in yourself first, so use your time and money wisely.

Be part of something bigger

> "I've come to believe that each of us has a personal calling that's as unique as a fingerprint – and that the best way to succeed is to discover what you love and then find a way to offer it to others in the form of service, working hard, and also allowing the energy of the universe to lead you."
> **– Oprah Winfrey**

You don't need another person to tell you that you are loved. No matter who you are or what abilities you have, you have worth and society will accept you for the value you bring to the world, so give back to it in your own ways.

Help the underprivileged, and through your acts of service you will see how blessed you are to be able to help others. When you find your path, you will find peace and contentment and you don't need to look for gratification – in any man or from anywhere else.

Be brave, humble and kind

> "One of the most courageous things you can
> do is identify yourself, know who you are,
> what you believe in and where you want to go."
> **– Sheila Murray Bethel**

Some people may think of women as weak, but you are not. Be strong and confident. Stand up for the abused and the oppressed. Learn and explore new things. For when you get out of your comfort zone, that's when you really grow. Learn how to negotiate. Don't be afraid to demand a pay that is worthy of the work you do. Believe in yourself.

Finally, always be humble and kind. Don't be afraid to own up to your mistakes and to learn from them. Listen to the voices of those around you – especially the marginalised – even if you do not have a solution. Sometimes, all they need is an empathetic ear to get through the day.

When you uphold these values as you grow up, you will certainly be beautiful women, and you don't need a podcast by any man to tell you that.

If you have been or are being sexually harassed or assaulted, the AWARE Women's Helpline (1 800 777 5555) provides assistance to callers with various concerns offering empathy, support, information and encouragement. It is run by women, for women.

Raising interracial children: Parents share challenges and opportunities

Three pairs of parents from different cultures talk about how they deal with the prejudices they face.

by Mirta Syazanna

The death in May 2020 of 46-year-old African-American George Floyd – who was pinned down by a police officer kneeling on his neck for more than eight minutes, despite protests from Floyd that he couldn't breathe – had sparked outrage in the US. It has also created a ripple effect felt all over the world, including Singapore.

When discrimination against minorities occur at different places and on different levels every other day – George Floyd, Ahmaud Arbery, the Christchurch mosque shootings, the perpetuation of racial stereotypes in Singapore, and the misappropriation of other cultures' dishes, among other incidents – we should ask ourselves as a society: How can we be better?

In Nelson Mandela's 1994 autobiography *Long Walk to Freedom*, the Nobel Peace Prize winner is quoted saying: "No one is born hating another person because of the color of his skin, or his background, or his religion. People must learn to hate, and if they can learn to hate, they can be taught to love, for love comes more naturally to the human heart than its opposite."

Although the father of post-apartheid South Africa was right in that no child is born racist, a 2017 study found that at around six months, the average infant automatically begins to distrust anything that looks and sounds different than their parents.

"Because most of us are born into monoracial environments we start to show preferences for own-race individuals, and then we start to show biases," said Kang Lee, a human development researcher at the University of Toronto.

So even if parents don't explicitly hate other ethnicities, they still need to teach children about tolerance and acceptance of other races and religions to temper naturally held biases.

But what about children who are raised in multiracial environments? The Pride speaks to mixed marriage couples on how they overcome challenges in their relationship and how they are teaching their interracial children to look beyond the colour of one's skin.

Discussing heritage and race is an open topic at home

30-year-old Singaporean Camille Tan-Mahendran – who is a Roman Catholic – first met her husband, 37-year-old Malaysian Mahendran – an Indian Hindu – seven years ago at a friend's bar while celebrating her brother's 18th birthday.

For Camille, she counts herself fortunate that her parents did not oppose the relationship from the start. Her mother simply kept mum as she journeyed with the couple in their blossoming relationship and even hung out with them regularly at the bar where Mahendran works.

She shares: "All over the world, people struggle through racial discrimination. Marrying a person with a darker skin tone will always be frowned upon. I had my worries that my family would find it hard to accept a person from a different race as my husband; we have our differences in every single aspect when it comes to faith and culture.

Camille and Mahendran at their wedding. *Credit: Camille Tan-Mahendran.*

A happy family: Camille, Kierann, Aarann and Mahendran.
Credit: Camille Tan-Mahendran.

"As a Chinese person, it is actually quite common to be raised with racial discrimination towards the minority race. Even now, you can still hear Chinese grandparents asking their grandkids to behave, if not *Apu neh neh* will catch. I believe that they don't know how sensitive and hurtful it is. It has become ingrained in our older folks from way back then.

"That said, I was never once swayed to follow and believe what my elders said. I grew up in a multiracial church and we never once segregated friendships due to skin tone or race. To me, racism does not naturally happen unless children learn from their elders and this should stop."

This is why the couple believes in making race and heritage an open topic in their home for their two sons, Kierann, six, and Aarann, three.

"Kierann would come home and ask why he is different from his friends and we are always happy to explain to him that he is perfectly blended with Indian and Chinese heritage. My older boy has tanner skin tone whereas Aarann is fairer. When we go out, it is quite typical of strangers to say things like 'Why are you so dark? *Didi* (younger brother) is fairer therefore he is more good looking.'.

"I used to rage because all these comments are unnecessary and these are comments that create racial issues. We often educate our boys and teach them to celebrate different cultural and religious festivities. It doesn't matter what colour our skin tone is because we are all beautiful and talented in our own ways," adds Camille.

The couple also recognises that having friends of different racial backgrounds helps children see that they are not alone and that there are many families like the Mahendrans and children like Kierann and Aarann. In 2017, the Mahendrans started Interracial Family Singapore, a community for all mixed families to unite and embrace diversity through events and family-centric activities.

Godparents of different races

Thirty-one-year-old Singaporean Rosemary Richard Sam, who is of Chinese and Indian heritage, has been married to her Nigerian husband, 35-year-old Ademola since 2014. They have two daughters, Ariel, six, and Iris, 10 months.

Rosemary shares her challenges before tying the knot: "Some of my relatives were happy and some were shocked and not so forthcoming, but we knew we wanted to spend the rest of our lives together and with my parents' blessing; no one else's opinion mattered. Today, the relatives who were not forthcoming see the love we have for each other, they have nothing but positive words to say.

"I've never seen race as an obstacle to getting to know someone better, I've always felt comfortable mixing around with people of any race. Upbringing is very important. It could have been how my parents, who are both Chindians as well, taught us the value and importance of respecting others," she adds.

Rosemary and Ademola with their daughters Ariel and Iris.
Credit: Rosemary Richard Sam.

While her kids are still too young to understand the differences in race, her eldest daughter has four godparents who are Chinese, Chinese-Malay, Punjabi and Indian.

To be adequately prepared when his daughters start learning Mandarin in school, Ademola is also learning the language.

At the same time, he also teaches his young girls Yoruba, the language from his hometown in Nigeria. This way, the couple ensures that Ariel and Iris are equally exposed to both languages and cultures.

Rosemary finds it very hard to understand why racial disharmony still exists in society. She says that she had to deal with racial discrimination from a young age, and now she has to watch her children face the same problems too.

She adds: "Society needs to see race as the human race and accept and learn the cultures because if they open up to it, they may open their minds to more interesting stuff."

Skin colour does not define us

On June 2, 2020, a father shared a poignant lesson with his daughter about race and nationality in a Facebook post which went viral.

A few months earlier, Lijesh Karunakaran's five-year-old daughter, Mayuki, came home asking her father if she was Singaporean. Her classmate had told her that she wasn't because of her darker skin.

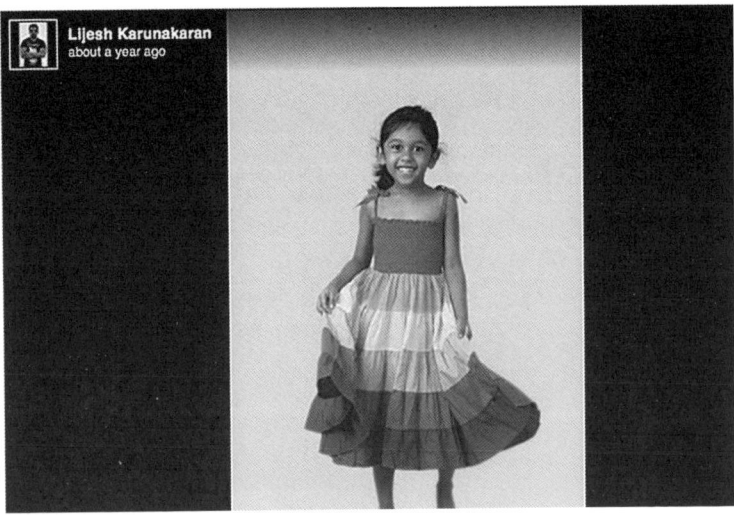

Credit: Facebook / Lijesh Karunakaran.

In another instance, Mayuki's class buddy – a classmate the teachers paired her with – refused to hold her hand, telling her that he was afraid of becoming "black" too.

In the past, Lijesh shared that he had to pause to think about what to say to his daughter. Eventually he explained that perhaps her classmate might not have known that unlike paint colours, skin colours don't mix.

A similar incident occurred while the pair was out shopping. A rainbow-coloured dress caught Mayuki's attention but unfortunately, it was not in her size. Before he could ask for the right size, the shop attendant passed him a pink dress and added, "We have it [the rainbow-coloured dress] in her size, but pink is nicer for her."

Even after Lijesh insisted that his daughter preferred the first dress, the woman replied, "Rainbow colours are very vibrant. Your daughter is dark. Take this pink one. This is nice for her."

He criticised the shop attendant for her insensitive comments, and father and daughter left the shop to buy the same dress at another outlet. Nevertheless, despite being happy with her new dress, the young girl still asked her father if pink was better for her.

"All colours look great on you. Pink, blue, white, black… all colours look good. But the rainbow colours look perfect! You look very beautiful in this," was his reply.

Through his post, netizens conveyed their support for the family and also shared similar incidents of such casual racism. One of them acknowledged how important parents are to help children understand and interpret the world around them.

It doesn't even have to be a big deal. Perhaps raising a child free of racism is a simple matter of getting the children accustomed to mingling with people of other races and cultures. Schools do a good job of educating children about race, culture and heritage, with events such as Racial Harmony Day. But even then, we should continue to teach our children about other cultural practices and religious beliefs to reduce their ignorance and debunk stereotypes of those who are not like them.

But it does begin with parents. Start by being welcoming to people of other races in their children's school, at the workplace or even in your neighbourhood – after all, we are our child's greatest role model.

The meaning of Christmas: A family that volunteers together gets the greatest gift of all

Parents teach their young children to help others, from welcoming strangers into their home to sewing stuffed toys for charity.

by Melissa Wong

No matter how busy we are, we still want to carve out family time together.

And one way families can spend quality time with one another is to volunteer together, like the Ng family.

Parents Eunice, a civil servant, and Alvin, a secondary school teacher, have made community service a priority, so much so that it has become a way of life for the rest of their family – eight-year-old Hannah and Timothy, six.

"The children see it as part of play. So, there's no line between running an errand to help someone out or going out to play," says Alvin, 38.

Some of the cards that the children made for the foreign domestic workers around their neighbourhood. *Credit: Eunice Chong.*

For example, during Mother's Day this year, the Ng's hearts went out to the foreign domestic workers (FDWs) here.

"I really felt for them during the circuit breaker because they were stuck looking after someone else's kids. They had their own kids at home and couldn't see them. We wrote cards and bought Mother's Day gifts to remind them they're loved and that their children appreciate all the things they were doing here," says Eunice, 39.

With their helper's assistance, the Ngs got the addresses of eight other FDWs and made surprise visits to deliver the gifts. Some of them were moved to tears, Eunice recalls.

This urge for philanthropy has been the driving force behind the Ngs even before their children arrived.

Reaching out

Alvin recalls a time while they were still dating: Eunice had read a news story about a cleaner who had lost her savings. She contacted the journalist, and next thing Alvin knew, the couple were on the way to the cleaner's – a complete stranger – flat to give her some money.

"It was then that I knew Eunice would feel moved to do such things," Alvin tells The Pride.

When Hannah was 18 months old and with Timothy on the way, the family helped to distribute bread at rental flats with Yong-en Care Centre, a charity arm of their church.

Some of the little tykes delivering bread at rental flats. Hannah is on the left.
Credit: Eunice Chong.

"Some flats had elderly living alone, some had very large families – but the elderly were very happy to see the little children. We did that once a month, until we moved on to other programmes," Alvin says.

So it was a natural progression for the kids to get more involved in their parents' volunteer work.

The true meaning of Christmas

Now, reaching out during the festive period has become a Christmas tradition for the Ngs.

In 2015, *The New Paper* published a story on two orphan boys who struggled to find joy during the festive season. Eunice tells The Pride: "They were estranged from their extended family and shared how it would get very lonely during the time of year. My heart really went out to them."

That was why Eunice and Alvin decided to invite the orphans to join them for Christmas that year. It was the first time anyone had reached out to the boys, and they accepted the Ngs' invitation as they were curious to see who would be so kind.

Though having strangers in the house felt awkward at first, they ended up sharing a lovely Christmas meal together. It was just something she felt she had to do, says Eunice.

Once, the family helped at their church's Christmas outreach programme where volunteers organised small parties in homes at Chinatown.

"We would ask residents if they would open up their homes and we would provide everything for the party. These are the homes that the church regularly reached out to, so we already knew them because they see us once a month," explains Alvin.

One party was held in a cramped two-room flat that housed a very large family. Joining the Ngs were other families with young children from their cell group.

One of the tougher moments, Eunice admits, was when Hannah, then four, started crying. It was stuffy and noisy, and she was tired and just wanted to leave. After the family got home, Eunice took the opportunity to impart important values to her daughter.

"We've been quite blessed. So, we make it a point to remind our children that Christmas is not just about presents, but to seek out opportunities that take us out of our comfort zone. Who wouldn't like a cosy party at home with loved ones, right? But I think there's more to Christmas," Eunice shares.

Nurturing children with empathy

Eunice tells The Pride how her son Timothy has a heart for the invisible; he notices people and things that others normally overlook. One of his favourite activities is greeting and befriending anyone and everyone, from estate cleaners to people washing their cars.

A couple of years ago, he befriended a cleaner at their estate, and invited him to his fourth birthday party. The cleaner, Uncle Sabuj, dressed up for the occasion and even brought a gift for the boy. In return, Uncle Sabuj invited the Ngs to where he lived, a large flat nearby shared by 14 tenants.

That same year, they packed goodie bags with snacks and toiletries and handed them out to cleaners on Christmas morning.

"The kids are aware that these things we do are very small and won't shake the foundation of society. But it still makes a difference to somebody," says Alvin. "I don't want the kids to grow up thinking that it's such a big problem and they can't do anything about it."

And the young siblings understand it well.

"We like helping because it encourages other people to help others too. It makes me happy," says Timothy.

Left: The children like to befriend cleaners around their estate. Right: Uncle Sabuj at Timothy's fourth birthday party. *Credit: Eunice Chong.*

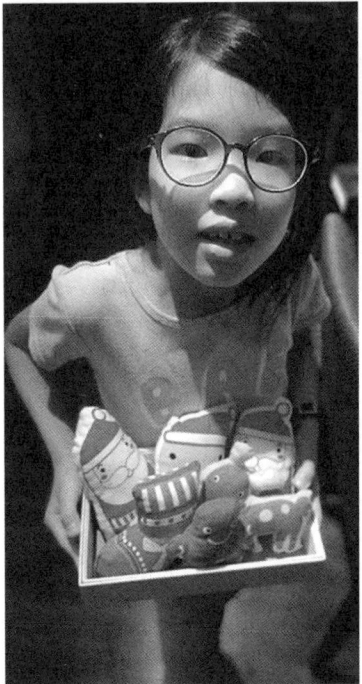 

Hannah with the stuffed animals she has sewn for charity (left picture). Volunteering together has made Hannah and Timothy fight less, say their parents (right picture). *Credit: Eunice Chong.*

"Helping others has made me more generous. And also helped me exercise my talents, like sewing and drawing," Hannah adds.

Currently, Hannah sews stuffed toys in support of Yong-en Care Centre. Paired with an endearing handwritten note, each of Hannah's handicrafts can be purchased with a minimum donation of $25.

Alvin posts her creations on his Facebook and when people ask to buy them, he directs them to the donation site so the Ngs don't handle any money directly. So far, Hannah has raised $560 for the centre.

Volunteering brings the family closer

There are many benefits to helping others as a family.

Not only do the little ones learn to be compassionate and selfless, it also helps them grow an interest in learning and moral responsibility.

Reaching out to others has also strengthened the relationship between Hannah and Timothy, says Eunice. The parents have noticed that they have an easier time resolving their children's quarrels, because from a young age, the kids are already used to seeing things from each other's perspective and caring about each other.

Eunice says: "They know intrinsically what is right and wrong, because they are exposed to these situations. It strengthens their sense of justice. So, when they run into issues, it's easier to appeal to that sense of morality. When you talk to them, you can see in their eyes that they already know."

And it's not just a one-way street either. Eunice and Alvin say that their children's pure-heartedness helps them to reflect on themselves.

"I sometimes ask myself why can Timmy befriend someone else so easily, whereas it's not the same for us. Why do we have so many barriers that prevent us from reaching out and have a conversation with someone from a different culture? That thought challenges me and makes me step out of my comfort zone," Eunice shares.

Start early, start small

Alvin and Eunice encourage parents to get their children acquainted with volunteering early, before they get too influenced by their peers.

"Children are naturally self-centred. Since Singapore is so affluent, there's a tendency for us to feel entitled to things. Everything is at our fingertips," Eunice explains.

"It's one thing to talk about it, and another thing to show them that other people do struggle. This way, we can teach them that we are not meant to keep our good circumstances only to benefit ourselves, but that we are blessed to be a blessing. It's important that they learn that from a young age."

It is important for children to see their parents model the life lessons – such as doing community service – that they are trying to teach, so that it gets normalised. But Eunice also cautions against being too aggressive about it.

She advises: "Don't push them too much and put them off. We've got to manage the opportunities. When they see there's a skill to be learnt or there's an element of play involved, they are happy to try something."

Look out for ways to help those around you

So are there many opportunities for families to volunteer together, even during Covid? Definitely, the couple agree.

"If we open our eyes, we see so many needs just right outside our door. Take a walk around the neighbourhood, or go to the rental blocks. It's not just about giving money, but rather developing friendships," says Eunice.

"As we grow as a society, we become more insular. We can give as much as we want, but at the end of the day, there are people who receive these gifts, but not have their emotional needs met. Little children are really good at satisfying these emotional bonds, more than adults are."

"The challenge is not so much finding needy people, but to overcome the notion that we should mind our own business. The tough part is normalising that altruistic behaviour," adds Alvin.

A family that volunteers together stays together, Alvin and Eunice with their children. *Credit: Eunice Chong.*

"It's important for our kids to not feel that what they're doing is unusual or exceptional. We don't want them to grow up thinking that they are special just because they help people.

"But perhaps if they grow up understanding that helping others is the norm – that it's normal to see a need and feel moved to fill it – and to encourage their friends to do the same – then we would have done our jobs as parents."

Being a good neighbour

How do we stop fuming over our neighbour's smoking habit?

He's smoking in his flat, but you suffer the ash and second-hand smoke in yours. How do you resolve the issue while keeping both sides happy?

by Jamie Wong

Cigarette ashes flutter into my kitchen window like autumn leaves into a cottage.

They land on the floor, forming black clumps that are warm to the touch. The smell of smoke stings my nostrils, and I know the same scent would perfume the clothes drying outside my window.

My neighbour, who lives directly above me, is smoking by his kitchen window again. What was a swell morning turns into a scene of chaos; I yank bamboo poles of clothing back indoors and rack them up, all while holding my breath and avoiding the hot ashes. It is an extreme sport.

If you think it's a small matter, I'm willing to bet that you don't have a neighbour who smokes.

I go to my friends for advice, and I realise that each of us has a unique solution to the problem.

Some get up in arms. "If I were you, I'd snap pictures of the ashes and go knock on their door!" To them, neighbours like these needed to be taught a lesson. After all, they have intruded into the sanctity of our home, and considering that most Singaporeans live on average about 10 years in their HDB flat before moving out, it's not something we can simply ignore.

Others prefer to invoke the authorities. "Just go there and be firm. Let them know that you'll inform the town council if they do it again," one of my friends suggested.

Someone I know even upped and moved away. Her previous neighbours smoked by their gates and windows, sometimes along the corridor near her unit. The smell never faded due to the frequent smoking and it haunted her family. They almost never opened their windows and front door, which was less than ideal in our hot weather. "My mum was driven to insanity over it," she joked.

Such experiences are so commonplace that when a ban on smoking at home was suggested in Parliament, it quickly became the talk of the town.

Some smokers were fuming, concerned about losing autonomy over what they can do at home. While they understood the implication of the intrusion, non-smokers favoured the idea due to health concerns or unpleasant experiences. Netizens hopped on to support the ban or suggest alternative solutions – like using cameras to catch those who smoke at home, setting up little "smoking zones" complete with air filters, or beefing up the resources to settle disputes.

Both sides bring up valid concerns. Yet one question remains: How do we get to the middle ground and gain a mutual understanding?

Keep calm and deal with it

We spend the day dealing with the world, and when evening rolls around, we look forward to putting our feet up and winding down. We just want to get by comfortably, so when someone steps on our toes we reflexively respond in anger.

But do we reach for the phone or knock on our neighbour's door too soon?

Perhaps it has happened three times this week and you are just so *done*. Or you are worried for someone in your household who has respiratory conditions. In a fit of annoyance, we forget that there is always the other side of the story.

Let's show some empathy. When non-smokers look at statistics like how six Singaporeans die from smoking-related conditions every day and how inhaling second-hand smoke can be as lethal as smoking itself, it is easy to wag a finger and judge without understanding.

Some smokers do it as a coping method to relieve frustration, loneliness, stress and anger. Most of the time, they are aware of the health risks, but are addicted to the habit. This results in smokers trapped in an endless cycle of dependency and despondency.

Smokers often begin smoking in their youth, influenced by peers or having older relatives who are smokers. Those who have smoked for decades often also believe that there is no turning back.

This by no means says that all smokers are in the wrong or that we must condone their habits just because they could be going through a rough patch. But it is worth considering your neighbour's situation just as much as your own.

So keep an open mind when approaching your neighbour. Some are considerate enough to change a few things, such as agreeing to smoke away from the window or balcony. Sometimes, you might realise that that inconsiderate person may actually be a friendly neighbour who just made an honest mistake.

But draw the line between silence and tolerance. My mother paid little mind to the ashes, saying that it didn't happen too often for her to be ruffled by it. She changed her mind when she got a whiff of my wardrobe days later, but it was too late by then. The damage had been done, and we had to toss the clothes back in the suds.

Finding the perfect balance

Many agree that a ban on smoking at home is a tad bit intrusive. While we can enlist the help of community mediation centres and town councils to facilitate a discussion, we need to approach the conflict with the right mindset.

> If you go in spoiling for a fight, even if the negotiation seems effective, it may end with both parties agreeing half-heartedly to terms they won't comply with anyway.

Adopt resolution skills; don't go in with preconceived notions. Ask questions that show curiosity rather than judgement. For example, a simple change from "You smoke at home and I don't like it" to "Is there anywhere else for you to smoke?" can prompt someone to engage in a constructive conversation.

Dealing with angry neighbours

Chances are, their frustration might not be directed at you; they may just be having a bad day and are not provoked by you. If so, remain patient and eventually they will come around. Of course, if the anger is directed at you, or they are simply too riled up to address the matter, back off gently and try again.

Generally speaking, it is better to speak to each other as neighbours first, before involving external agencies. There are avenues for additional help. Complaints to the National Environment Agency or the police may feel like an easy choice, but it shouldn't be the first resort, as this can spark off misunderstandings.

For both sides of the debate, the point is to keep trying to understand the alternative point of view, even when the other party gets aggressive. For an effective way to resolve conflicts with their neighbours, everyone should take a walk in each other's shoes.

Non-smokers, remember that you're not there to instantly flip their perspective around and make them stop smoking at home there and then. For smokers, remember that it takes courage for your neighbour to broach an uncomfortable subject. Be mindful that both sides have concerns and wants – the key is to be open to negotiation.

With that in mind, you can bet I'll be knocking on my neighbour's door with my smoke-infused dri-fit tee, not to tell them to smoke less, but simply to find out more.

Would you invite a homeless person to stay in your home?

He wants to rekindle the kampung spirit by getting Singaporeans to open their homes to those in need.

by Lianne Ong

He opens his home to strangers who are going through difficult times.

Since he moved into his four-room HDB flat in a mature estate, Kenneth Heng and his wife Zi Ying have hosted people in need – from a youth who fell out with his family, to a Pakistani family who travelled to Singapore for their son's cancer treatment.

Kenneth and his wife had learnt about a 24-year-old Pakistani man, E, who had stage 4 rectal cancer and was in Singapore seeking

Kenneth (right) and his wife Zi Ying (far left) hosted a Pakistani man, E (seen in the background) and his family during his cancer treatment in 2018. *Credit: Kenneth Heng.*

treatment, accompanied by his mother. Initially, they stayed in a hostel. However, the hostel could only accommodate them for a month and the treatment was three months long.

As his flat was next to a lift lobby and five minutes from the hospital, their home was ideal for the Pakistani family. They agreed on the living arrangements, and E and his mother moved in a few days before Christmas in 2018.

E's mother's way of showing her gratefulness and love was to regularly cook up a storm in the kitchen.

"It was a test of our Singaporean inclinations for order and cleanliness, but with language being a barrier, it was challenging to communicate this to his mother," Kenneth recalls.

Sadly, a few days after a joyous Christmas celebration together, E passed away suddenly. Together with friends, Kenneth helped to work out the administrative arrangements and cover the costs of the repatriation. The couple took turns to spend time with E's mother as she grieved.

Kenneth says: "We could not imagine how difficult it would have been if E and his mother had not found anybody they could trust in Singapore. We saw our neighbours and friends step forward to render support too."

Starting a network of open homes

But Kenneth, 31, isn't content with opening just his home to others. With Abraham Yeo of Homeless Hearts of Singapore, he started the Open Home Network (OHN) in June 2020. It is a ground-up, community project that aims to educate and equip families to offer shelter to those who are in trouble, Kenneth tells The Pride.

"It is a very direct expression of helping the homeless by galvanising and preparing families to open their homes to persons who are experiencing crisis," explains Kenneth, who is the founder of Solve n+1, a social enterprise.

OHN is a collaboration with Homeless Hearts and A Safe Place, two organisations that work with the homeless in Singapore. OHN operates alongside family service centres and assists social workers in finding a host family for the person-in-crisis, and is run largely by volunteers.

A ground-up initiative to help the homeless

Offering your home as a shelter to a stranger rent-free does come with valid concerns, so OHN focuses on educating and preparing host families.

"We encourage potential host families to speak with every member of their household to make sure everyone is comfortable with the idea, and to talk to their friends to get their buy-in as well," Kenneth tells The Pride.

The recruitment process is designed to get every family to understand what hosting entails. These are done through modules sent via WhatsApp, with narratives to explain and questions for them to consider.

There are some fundamentals OHN sticks to, says Kenneth. "We don't want to be too prescriptive about hosting to ensure that they understand that hosting is person-focused. Every person is unique, every crisis is unique, and every time support is rendered, it will be different."

When it started in June, OHN appealed for families to come forward if they were willing to extend their hospitality to those who were seeking refuge and a safe place to stay. At first, 160 families expressed interest. However, these were whittled down to 10 families after they went through the rigorous recruitment process.

Explains Kenneth: "We see this as a good thing because they are thinking seriously about what it takes to host someone. If you're not prepared, you could walk away from this experience feeling like a failure."

Since then, OHN sees about one new family a week stepping forward to offer their space. Currently there are 13 families actively hosting, says Kenneth.

Host concerns

The most common question the OHN team gets is: "How long do I have to host?"

This is where the OHN team tries to orientate host families to a different mindset, says Heng. While they try to facilitate stays to be from six months to a year, there is no hard and fast answer to this because of the nature of the crisis each person faces.

Kenneth Heng who helped set up the Open Home Network (OHN). *Credit: Kenneth Heng.*

Many of the problems and broken relationships that drove them away from their homes are not easily resolved.

"We try to focus on building relationships instead," Kenneth says.

During the recruitment process, some families start off with much enthusiasm, ready to transform their spare room into a hotel-standard guest room. This is where OHN case workers would try to help them understand that the people seeking help tend to come from unsafe homes, and have no reference point as to what a stable home looks like. So while setting up a comfortable place is part of the deal, the emphasis is more on providing a safe space to stay.

In other words, it is more important to prepare an emotional haven rather than physical space.

There are also others who assume that to host a person requires a big house. That's not always true. Kenneth says OHN has a family of six living in a five-room HDB flat offering to be a host.

"Sometimes an openness of heart is all that is needed – even if it's just a couch or a tatami mat."

The key to matching a host family to the person who needs help goes beyond the type of dwelling, of course.

"It's like dating. No one holds hands on the first date. It can take up to three meet-ups between the host family and beneficiary for them to decide on whether it is a comfortable fit," says Kenneth.

Host families come from different religious and racial backgrounds, and dwelling types range from landed property to three-room flats. The youngest person OHN has helped is 18 and the oldest is 70.

Explains Kenneth: "We don't have a first-come-first-served approach, we try to match according to who we think will benefit from the relationship the most. Some families are more suited to supporting a youth because they are more wired that way, while some have a heart for the elderly."

Staying with host families is free, though many do want to pay for some part of their lodging. This is negotiated between the two parties, based on their relationship and mutual understanding. For example, the person could pay for their share of the utilities if they are working and drawing a salary. "This really depends on the relationship they have with the host – we try not to influence how this turns out," Kenneth says.

Recreating the kampung spirit

While OHN was started as part of a bigger programme called the Bezer Initiative, Kenneth's efforts are a result of his wanting to rekindle the kampung spirit that was abundant in pre-independent Singapore.

"Things were more communal back then. It allowed us as a nation to be strong because we shared in each other's problems. A lot has changed due to affluence, and it is challenging to have communal living with the structure we have today."

He says: "I got to know my neighbours when I borrowed their can opener. That was how I started a conversation with them."

Now, Kenneth sometimes helps his neighbour's children with their homework and the couple, who have no children, occasionally get a free meal when the neighbours cook some extra food.

"That's the kampung spirit that we lack today in most of Singapore," says Kenneth. "We want to recreate a 21st-century kampung even though we live behind concrete walls. That's the heart of what we try to establish with all our families."

Before OHN started, Kenneth spent a year putting together a community White Paper on this initiative. Homelessness is a complicated issue – even the term "homeless" is a bit of a misnomer as many who sleep rough actually have an address on their identity card.

But there are many reasons why they don't or can't live at their official residence, as "their own home is no longer a safe one," Kenneth says.

The people OHN has helped have wide-ranging reasons for not being able to live in their home – domestic violence, mothers with unsupported pregnancies and hoarding families are just some of them.

It is these "invisible homeless" that are not covered by any comprehensive study so far and Kenneth hopes that more data will become available. "The family violence cases are so severe, I wonder how long it took to get to this level. If these persons had friends to help them in the past, would they have been able to intervene?"

Currently, OHN's referrals are growing but its list of host families is insufficient to meet the demand. Those that do not get matched to a host family are referred to shelters, such as Safe Sound Sleeping Places (S3Ps), or homes. And OHN is putting out the call for more host families.

"As long as we have homes, we will be open for as long as we can," says Kenneth.

"Maybe it all starts with borrowing a can opener, or cooking an extra portion of a meal to share with your neighbour. I think when we start there, then open homes become less far-fetched."

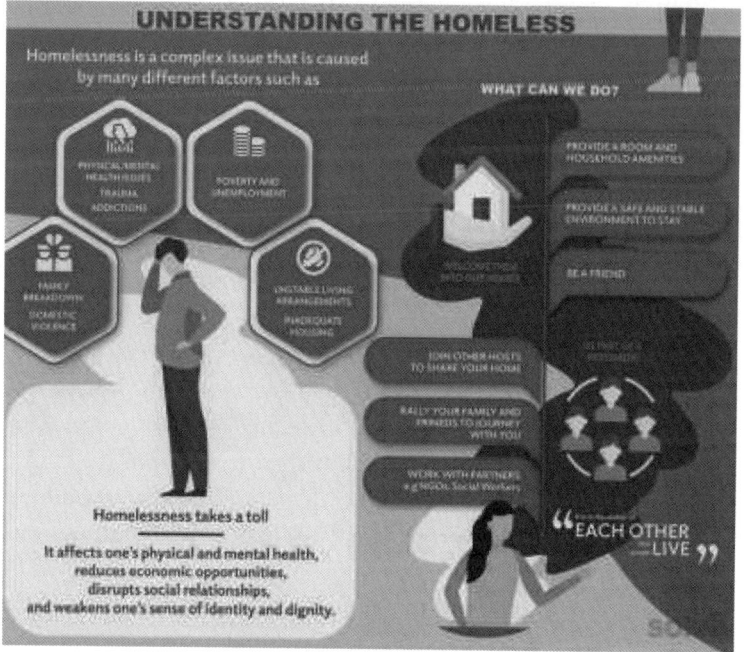

Graphic explaining the concept of being homeless. *Credit: Solve n+1.*

What would you do with crying kids while working from home?

A mum decided to fire back at a neighbour who complained about her crying baby.

by Mirta Syazanna

Just the other day, my two daughters (ages four and five) got into a screaming match after one of their usual evening showers. My younger one had accused her sister of not using soap to bathe while my elder one, full of righteous indignation at the wrongful accusation, had screamed back at her. Both of them were fixed in an intense stare-off for a good five minutes.

In the corner, my husband and I were stifling our laughter, because how often do you hear little girls say "I'm angry with you" in such utter seriousness? We had decided in the moment that we were going to let our daughters resolve their own problems with each other.

We were mirroring *mimamoru*, a Japanese "hands-off" childcare techniques, that is being practised in the girls' preschool. Instead of intervening in every situation, *mimamoru* or "watching over" encourages parents to allow their children to work things out on their own.

While all the back and forth shouting was going on, I was wondering at the back of my mind if the high-pitched voices were able to penetrate the walls of my HDB flat. It was 7pm (not quite the quiet hours of 10.30pm to 7am yet), and my doors and windows were all shut, but I still worried if my neighbours would think I was abusing my children.

Recently, a Singapore mum shared on Facebook that her neighbour complained that her five-month-old baby was crying too loudly and disturbing them while they were working from home.

According to Geralyn Yeh, the neighbour asked her to close her main door during the day. She also posted the unsigned handwritten note, which urged her to be more considerate.

Geralyn shared that the neighbour had come over to shout at her helper about the baby's cries while she was not home.

In her Facebook post, she said that in return, she wrote a letter to the neighbour to explain the situation. In it, she highlighted that crying is a baby's natural way of communicating its needs.

"For infants, they can get real irritating with their high pitch screaming or crying but that's the way they communicate and I do not have the magic to stop her from crying or make her grow up faster so that she can communicate without crying (sic)," she wrote.

The mother continued to pepper the letter with sarcastic remarks such as giving her baby "a stern warning" and asking the neighbour to contact NEA, HDB or the police for other suggestions to cope with the noise.

She signed off the letter, reaffirming her view of the situation, as the "parent of the innocent child".

On a Reddit thread – which garnered over 300 comments – about this incident, many Redditors compared a crying baby to renovation work.

Hikarimo98 wrote: "I was doing my test online at home. And guess what? A… drill rammed through the air for two hours. Raging but helpless."

Some thought the neighbour should calm down but still gave her the benefit of the doubt.

ChoiceScarfMienfoo wrote: "I felt bad for everyone involved including the suffering neighbour until I saw that they had gone to shout at the helper. Hello the helper is innocent one, not even the parents leh, you shout for ****, power trip is it? Settle it amicably la."

Sanguineuphoria added: "Parent sounds very pissed off so I would take it with a pinch of salt. Maybe neighbour poked their head through the open door like "hey could you keep it down!!" = shouting/scolding. Idk what the neighbour said also."

Some Redditors, however, wondered if Geralyn had overreacted.

Sputnikcosmo wrote: "I have not lived in Singapore long enough to understand the culture. But in any part of the world,

I would believe that the right thing to do was to check on the neighbour to see if there is something wrong with the baby and if they need any help.

"If it is repeated, it may be a good idea to speak personally in the right tone to explain about the impact on the work and see if there is something that can be done about this. Also, explain that I have already explored having a headphone. I would also think that it is quite OK to have some disturbance while WFH and it is expected that work will be impacted.

"The letter above is also in the wrong spirit. I would have just written that I am sorry for the inconvenience but happy to discuss ways in which we can address this. And that is possible only if you show up and speak and not remain anonymous. And if not, please feel free to report or speak to the police to see if they have any suggestions.

"Sarcasm deteriorates the situation more than anything else."

Agreeing, Redditor e-tunnelsunshine chimed in: "Totally agree with this. Just from reading this letter, I'd think a reasonable solution would be for the parents to shut their doors but open their windows (like most households do). And any sound that comes through even after closing the door needs to be understood, can't stop a baby from crying!

"Both the neighbour and the parents did not handle this well… All that rage and sarcasm. Of course, we don't know what exactly happened but just by judging from this I don't think either party reacted well!"

One Redditor, rekabre, warned of entitled parents: "Most everyone here seemed so supportive of the mother and applauding her response but I felt the 'suck it up' and 'how dare you complain' attitude just seemed like the usual entitled parent.

"No matter how much you 'can't help' (it's subjective) the problem, you can't just dismiss the other people suffering your problem."

Kindness is a two-way street

Personally, I am glad I live in a young estate with neighbours who are around my age and understand the challenges of being a parent with young children.

I have neighbours who have a seven-year-old on the autistic spectrum. Every other day, I can hear her screaming. However, it lasts only a few minutes.

Sometimes, I can also hear some of my neighbours' young kids crying and being reprimanded by their parents. Some of my neighbours have confessed to me that they have sometimes left their crying children out in the corridor to teach them a lesson. Similarly, I have also done my fair share of leaving my kids outside my door (just for a few minutes) if they get out of hand.

Thus, on top of the usual shriek of planes flying over my estate during the day, I have become accustomed to loud noises. My solution usually is to plug in my headphones when working from home.

Kindness is a two-way street filled with tolerance and empathy. Judging or jumping to conclusions without first understanding the other party's situation and challenges is a recipe for disharmony. As fellow residents, it also makes our home environment less pleasant if we have to tiptoe around neighbours we have problems with.

In my case, I'm glad my doors were closed that day when I was "practising" *mimamoru* with my children. Because even though I know my neighbours won't complain, with all of us accustomed to constantly being around children, I think they deserve to enjoy what little peace they can get.

I know that they would do the same for me.

I discovered the kampung spirit in an online gathering with total strangers

Many people say the kampung spirit is dead. But I caught a glimpse of it connecting with others through meaningful conversations.

by Serene Leong

"So you're going for group therapy," quipped a colleague when he heard that I would be joining an online gathering to connect with others in my neighbourhood.

"It's just getting to know my neighbours," I replied in amusement.

I'd chanced upon FriendzoneSG from an article on the rise of sharing sessions with strangers to promote mental well-being during Covid-19, and was intrigued by its idea of recreating the kampung spirit online.

Having moved into my neighbourhood not long ago, I don't know many residents. I do know neighbours living on my floor – we'd exchange friendly greetings when we see each other or food on occasion, but our interactions never went beyond casual conversation.

So, with a lot of free time on my hands, I thought why not sign up for a session?

I could get to know new neighbours who share similar interests, or at the very least, lend a listening ear to someone.

FriendzoneSG is a community-building organisation dedicated to creating a culture of connectedness and care through meaningful conversations. The founders believe everyone has something to give and receive, and that Singapore is full of diverse and interesting people who just haven't met yet.

Co-founders Grace Chua and Valencia Wong tell The Pride that when they were in university, they loved the vibrancy of campus life – there were invitations to play sports, neighbours surprising each other with fruits and bubble tea or leaving encouraging notes during stressful times – but saw a lack of a young adult community in their neighbourhoods after graduating.

FriendzoneSG was born out of an inspiration to recreate that connection and to give more opportunities for young people who live in the same area to connect meaningfully.

Their dream: A nation where friendliness is the norm and people don't feel alone.

"It's hard for people to care for their neighbours without first feeling some sense of belonging in their neighbourhoods. We see our role as creating the space for those friendships to be formed," says Grace.

She adds that they hope to create communities beyond neighbourhoods and across generations. Part of this involves raising community connectors – people who care about deepening friendships and can share their passions, networks, resources, experiences and stories with others.

Initially, gatherings were held at void decks adorned with fairy lights, fluffy carpets and cushions for a cosy ambience. But since Covid-19, all gatherings have been taken online.

A FriendzoneSG neighbourhood gathering before the circuit breaker.
Credit: Facebook / FriendzoneSG.

A Zoom session with FriendzoneSG. *Credit: Facebook / FriendzoneSG.*

Connecting through meaningful conversations

On the day of the gathering, I logged on punctually at 1pm. By now, I'm used to Zoom meetings, so this was not a new experience. What was new perhaps was that in the virtual room of about 20 people, I didn't know anyone.

However, Grace and Valencia quickly put us at ease by explaining how the session would work.

The purpose, they said, was to "Make new friends. Be yourself. Be open to listen to different perspectives."

Those were the three things I tried to keep in mind as we broke out into smaller groups. Thankfully, there were guided questions to help steer and keep the conversation going, reducing any potential awkward silences which are part and parcel of meeting new people for the first time.

In the next half hour, my group talked about experiences in our neighbourhood, what we have been doing during the circuit breaker and questions that are weighing on our minds.

Who knew that despite differences in ages and life stages – some are working, others studying; some are single, others in a relationship – we all had something to contribute and take away!

Sharing personal experiences

I could see my group mates nodding their heads in agreement as I talked about the boredom of staying home and not doing anything meaningful to pass the time; the struggle to maintain my sanity as circuit breaker days blur into weeks and months.

Amanda, one of the participants, said: "I will set goals to avoid one day going to the next, for example, fitness goals, or how many books I want to read, or courses I want to take. It helps jerk myself out of watching TV."

Another participant, Diane, agreed that it is not healthy to keep scrolling through Instagram or binge-watching Netflix and shared that she has been cooking more since the circuit breaker began.

A third, Keith, suggested learning a new hobby. He had recently started playing the piano again after having not touched it for a long time.

One participant, Jade, admitted that she has been wanting to volunteer but never actively pursued it. She said that the conversations she had with the group inspired her to start volunteering!

Being one of the older ones in my group, I was more than happy to give advice and support regarding various topics on relationships and work.

I told an undergraduate who is now working as an intern not to worry about finding a dream job immediately after graduation as it

(From left) FriendzoneSG co-founders Grace, Tham and Valencia. *Credit: Facebook / FriendzoneSG.*

takes time to figure out what one wants to do. I told her, instead, to view the process as a learning experience. I also shared with the group that the people you work with is just as important as the work you do when looking for the right job.

Building social capital and bridging social isolation

What was my biggest takeaway from the session?

I realised that we are social creatures with a need for connection. Acknowledging this is the first step to reaching out to our fellow friends and neighbours.

Knowing that we are all experiencing the same emotions, struggles and challenges in the new normal of Covid-19 helps me feel less alone.

Many people say the kampung spirit is dead. But I disagree.

Because I caught a glimpse of it during my group conversations. In a form I would not have expected.

Instead of sharing food like our grandparents did in the old kampung days, we shared ideas and knowledge that are just as, if not, more valuable.

As I reflect on Valencia's final words: "Community is yours to create", I realised that it is our choice to reach out to our friends and neighbours, even while keeping a safe physical distance. There are many ways and platforms to connect if we are willing to make the effort.

The FriendzoneSG team encourages participants to continue conversations on Telegram. In my group, we have been sharing food recommendations in our area and even photos of the beautiful sunset from our windows on the last day of the circuit breaker!

The session made me wonder if there are friends whom I have neglected in the past few weeks and reminded me to check in on them or perhaps even surprise them with a special delivery.

Settling into the new normal has been difficult, but our shared experiences can help us to overcome these challenges together.

Coming together to help others

Childhood cancer survivor works two jobs during Covid-19, volunteers to help the needy

23-year-old cancer survivor works two jobs to help family, yet still finds time to help less fortunate during Covid-19 difficulties.

by Melissa Wong

Life hasn't been the easiest for 23-year-old Nazri Arshad.

During the circuit breaker, both his parents lost their jobs as cleaners in a condominium. So the Pastry & Baking student at ITE College took on part-time jobs during the circuit breaker – a food delivery rider by day and packer by night – to help his family make ends meet.

Nazri Arshad found time to give back to the community despite his personal struggles. *Credit: Nazri Arshad.*

Despite his hardships, Nazri still found time to give back during the recent Hari Raya festivities.

With what little he had, he baked and sent Raya cookies to families like his who were going through a tough time during the pandemic. He even got his delivery rider friends, whom he knew had lost their jobs during the circuit breaker, to deliver the cookies so they could earn the extra income.

But his generosity isn't the only thing that makes Nazri special.

The reason Nazri is still in school now is that in 2013, when he was 16, he was diagnosed with leukaemia.

A relentless high fever had sent him to hospital for a month before the doctors finally diagnosed him with a rare condition called acute undifferentiated leukaemia and moved him from the neurology ward to the paediatric oncology ward.

Back then, his parents struggled to be the beacon of strength and courage for him, Nazri says. He recounts how he saw his mother in tears, grappling with the reality that was in front of her. That scene gave him the resolution to endure his condition, and he ended up comforting his parents instead.

Nazri tells The Pride: "To be honest, some people would be crying and upset about this, but for me, I didn't feel anything. I just feel that this is just a test from God, and that I just need to respect what He is asking me to go through. I believe that if God wants to take you through this experience, He will guide you. It's important to think positive!"

What worried Nazri the most was having to miss out on his studies. So, that was the very thing his mother used to motivate him throughout his one-year stay at the hospital undergoing chemotherapy and seven surgeries – to recover as fast as he could so that he could return to school.

Both mother and son share an exceptional bond. One year into treatment, Nazri received a bone marrow donation from his mother. But the post-surgery period proved to be the toughest time of his healing journey. Stuck in an isolation ward for a month, he was kept away from people, and worst of all, could not see his mum.

Nazri shares: "When my mother was not around and at another hospital after giving me her bone marrow, I felt very lonely. I cried a lot. But after crying, I felt better and reminded myself to think positively."

Presently, Nazri has been in remission for the past five years. In 2015, he finished treatment and was declared cancer-free. He went back to school and he is looking forward to graduating in 2021 with a certification in Pastry & Baking.

His optimism has played a big part in helping him beat the illness. Despite hurtful comments from a fair share of his friends, Nazri's indomitability has allowed him to look past their ignorance.

—

"I had a friend tell me, 'Go away, I'm scared you'll pass your virus to me'. And another said, 'Oh, I thought you died already'. But I ignored them. I refuse to allow their words to get into my head."

—

While caring for him, both of Nazri's parents lost their cleaning jobs. Although they received support from the Children's Cancer Foundation (CCF) and other sources of financial assistance, life was still hard for the family.

According to a CCF spokesman, many people still don't know much about cancer and as a result, do not give patients or survivors the kindness and fair treatment they deserve. For example, it is crucial to understand that cancer, unlike a virus, is not infectious.

Another common misconception is why children undergoing cancer treatment wear masks.

We wear masks in public now in the new Covid-19 normal not only to protect ourselves from catching the virus, but also to stop ourselves from infecting others if we do have the disease.

The reason why children undergoing cancer treatments wear masks is to protect themselves from viruses and infections as they have a lowered immune system, and not because they have something contagious.

A giving heart

Covid-19 and the circuit breaker have made life tougher for Nazri and his parents but he remains positive despite having to work from morning to night, while making time for his studies.

Instead of fixating on his own problems, he prefers to focus on helping other people in need. During Ramadan, Nazri started a

Coming together to help others 147

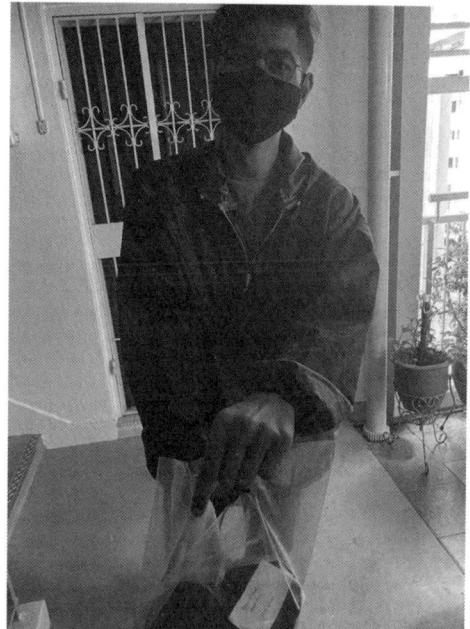

Nazri delivering Hari Raya cookies to families who had lost their income. *Credit: Nazri Arshad.*

charity project where he baked Raya cookies for families who had lost their income. Knowing that people's spirits were dampened due to the circuit breaker and the Hari Raya Bazaar being called off, Nazri wanted to bring cheer to those who could not even afford Raya cookies for their families at home.

He tells The Pride: "I put on social media that I was doing a baking donation and I ended up giving cookies to 30 families all over Singapore. I got my food delivery friends to help deliver to the farther parts of Singapore and I paid them. Some families wondered why I didn't deliver all the cookies by myself, because they wanted to thank me personally, but I couldn't reach 30 homes myself in just one or two days!"

Nazri paid for the ingredients and the deliveries himself, and he would have it no other way. He explains: "A few families asked if they could pay me, but I told them to donate directly to CCF or Ain Society instead. I refused their money because my aim is to help people. Many of my friends said I was wasting my money, but I told them that I didn't think of it that way."

And his charity isn't a one-off either. Right now, Nazri is saving to buy groceries for those who can't afford them. He explains that when he was younger, his mother told him that although some people are smiling on the surface, they may still be going through a lot and may not even have food to eat. So, whenever he can, Nazri approaches his local community centre for the contacts of needy families, then visits them with a bag of groceries.

His heart of gold does not come from a wallet of plenty. In fact, quite the opposite. It was Nazri's tough childhood that inspired him to extend a helping hand to those going through hardship.

"When I was in Primary 1, we lost our HDB flat because we couldn't afford to pay for it. So, my family lived on the beach. My parents had to send me to school every day and I could see how difficult it was for them. There were other families living at the beach too, some even with small children and babies.

Life was very tough, but my experience growing up made me who I am and made me more mature. I always think that if life were to become easier for me, I still need to remember my past and where I came from."

A community to be grateful for

Another part of Nazri's past that has helped him become the young man he is today, is the staff at CCF and nurses at KK Women's and Children's Hospital (KKH). Till today, he still calls them his "second family". Throughout the two years that Nazri spent in and out of hospital, they were with him every step of the way.

The Family Resource Centre at KKH is a playroom with games and books where Nazri would visit if he felt well enough. Each time, CCF volunteers would be there if he needed someone to talk to or play with, something he is incredibly grateful for.

Aside from emotional support, CCF has also helped Nazri financially with his medical, transport, school, food and maintenance needs. It was especially supportive in back-to-school support, organising sessions with his school to discuss Nazri's learning and schooling needs in view of his medical condition. CCF also gave him bursary awards for three years.

Typical of Nazri, he didn't want to just be a beneficiary. In 2018, he volunteered to help out at CCF's Survivor's Day and End of Treatment Party celebrations, and also took part in both local and overseas volunteering projects organised by the foundation.

He explains: "When I volunteer, I can meet new people and hear their own stories. I feel encouraged hearing their stories, especially since we've all been through similar things. Every word and encouragement from them, no matter how small, was meaningful to me and I am very grateful.

"But my favourite part is visiting cancer patients at the hospital – sharing my story with them and reassuring them, and also encouraging the parents and giving them hope."

One of the activites organised under The Hope Train programme.
Credit: Children's Cancer Foundation.

Right now, Nazri works as a food delivery rider and intends to continue doing so even after school starts while his parents look for jobs. In view of declining donations faced by CCF, he has also volunteered to be part of its online fundraising campaign, The Hope Train, to help raise more funds and childhood cancer awareness.

Nazri's hope is that his story can encourage other people going through what he did, and help them feel that they are not alone.

"Face your problem, don't run away from it. Because that is the only way you can conquer it."

Would you like to learn how to cook from this 85-year-old great grandma?

Nursing home starts Facebook Live cooking series to show how persons with dementia can still lead empowering lives.

by Jamie Wong

Madam See's wrinkled hands move with grace, skillfully packing the pandan leaves into her palm and fastening the bundle in one masterful knot.

Saturday morning sunlight filters through the spacious common area in the Home of Gerbera, where the 85-year-old resident of Apex Harmony Lodge is minutes away from kicking off her first live cooking demonstration on Facebook. "Just fold it like this," she instructs in Mandarin, "so you don't need to chop up a mess."

Observing Madam See, you wouldn't be faulted for assuming that she is just like any other grandmother (she's a great-grandmother, actually) preparing a well-loved recipe in the kitchen.

Madam See (left) and the ingredients for her cooking lesson (right). *Credit: Ng Wei Xuan.*

This is exactly what the Facebook livestream is meant to show, says Ng Wei Xuan, 29, who leads the community engagement team at Apex Harmony Lodge.

"When you think of elderly persons with dementia, you think angry, moody, temperamental. But you don't see many of those stereotypes here, as we have always been looking for ways to empower them."

With him are deputy CEO Kah Wei and some colleagues on hand to monitor and assist in the livestream, titled Grandma's Kitchen.

Despite being diagnosed with dementia, the residents at the lodge still retain their mannerisms and characteristics. For example, Kah Wei tells The Pride, Madam See is a woman of efficiency, which can be seen in her emphasis on cooking with minimal clutter.

Common symptoms of dementia include memory loss, language problems, misplacing things and withdrawal from social activities. Persons with dementia may struggle with basic tasks such as putting on clothes, finding their way in familiar places, or staying on topic in a conversation.

For caregivers, it is recommended that they help dementia sufferers maintain daily routines to encourage independence. For example, caregivers can label household items, put tripping hazards away and lay out the clothes that are to be worn – all these allow dementia sufferers to comfortably take care of their own needs.

As of June 2020 in Singapore, there are almost 615,000 people aged 65 and above, an increase of 5.6% from the same period the previous year. An IMH study in 2015 found that up to one in 10 people in Singapore aged 60 and above may have dementia. In other words, with Singapore's rapidly ageing population, dementia may be a societal issue that will affect us more and more in the coming years.

Dedicated home for dementia

Tucked away among a quiet neighbourhood in Pasir Ris, Apex Harmony Lodge is the first and only nursing home specifically for persons with dementia. Set up in 1999, the home has undergone a transformation within the last five years to better serve their residents and the dementia community at large.

Residents having lunch at the common area of Apex Harmony Lodge. *Credit: Ng Wei Xuan.*

For World Alzheimer's Month, the home went on Facebook Live with an empowering series of cooking shows featuring their residents sharing their recipes and life stories. The Pride had the pleasure of being present during the live debut.

The first session has Madam See sharing her homemade *ondeh-ondeh* recipe. Married into a Peranakan family when she was 24, she learnt to make it from observing her mother-in-law, who sold the snack. Of the family's four daughters, only she mastered it. "For a family of ten, I'll make over two kilograms of this snack," she said.

When the live session starts, Madam See confidently takes charge, rolling the dough out easily as she shares nuggets of wisdom on good work ethic and business morals.

Sometimes she combines both together: "If you're running a big business, you have to make enough for everyone, and you have to make it fast."

Despite her natural business acumen, Madam See reveals that she has never sold her homemade *ondeh-ondeh* and always gave it away. She fondly recalls how popular it was among children.

"Children love these, so I always made as much as I could," she says in Mandarin.

Live show host and community engagement executive Su Yin, 32, banters cheerfully with Madam See and translates some of her witticisms for the viewers. She teases Madam See in Mandarin, gesturing at Kah Wei, who is off camera, "You're making *ondeh-ondeh* for the boss today, can you do a beautiful job?"

Madam See laughs, before confidently replying in Mandarin: "Sure! Why can't I?"

As they chatter on camera, a fragrant pandan scent wafts through the home, drawing the attention of other residents. A fellow resident gets to do a taste test, and gives Madam See an encouraging thumbs-up and a slice of wisdom of her own. "If someone makes food for you, you should show gratitude," she says wisely in Mandarin.

It is this sense of casual friendship that helps build a welcoming environment.

"We have always worked towards empowering persons with dementia," Wei Xuan tells The Pride. "We do our best to make it happen, right down to setting the right environment and using the correct terminology."

Volunteers and staff at Apex Harmony Lodge adopt the approach of finding out more about the person with dementia, assisting them in their strengths, potentials and interests. Explains Wei Xuan: "We have very intense routines for helping the elderly here, we go deep into their likes and dislikes and we review them every six months."

Even as the session draws to a close, Madam See insists on making enough *ondeh-ondeh* for everyone at the lodge, and the livestream ends on a cheerful note as residents tuck into the freshly prepared snack at the well-furnished common area, decorated with plants and residents' artwork.

Su Yin (left), Madam See and another staff member waving hello to viewers at the start of the livestream. *Credit: Facebook / Apex Harmony Lodge.*

Off camera, we watch the staff interact with the residents, laughing and chatting freely over the boiling pandan-infused water as they continue making the *ondeh-ondeh*.

Wei Xuan tells The Pride that the Facebook Live series is one of the many initiatives created to give the home's residents independence. Past initiatives include allowing residents to work at a laundromat and volunteer at orphanages.

"We want to redefine what caring for the elderly means by assisting the residents to contribute and express themselves in their own ways," Wei Xuan says.

Satisfied with her work, Madam See waves at the camera. "Alright, thank you everyone… see you next time, we'll do it again!"

Animal lovers come together to rescue hamsters, guinea pigs and chickens

Animal welfare advocates set up groups for less common pets to tackle abuse and increase pet care standards.

by Lianne Ong

Think of pet rescue and chances are, your thoughts would stray towards dogs and cats and groups like Save Our Street Dogs and Cat Welfare Society.

And while organisations like SPCA and Acres cater to all animals large and small, a new generation of animal rescue and advocacy groups have sprung up in the last two years and are still going strong.

These newer groups, started through Facebook interest groups, focus on less popular pets such as hamsters, guinea pigs and yes, even chickens!

Even though these groups have continued to work through the pandemic, Covid-19 has made it more challenging, as it has hampered their public education efforts.

At the same time, the need for rescue, foster care and rehoming of these animals has been magnified, as more cases of abuse and abandonment emerge.

Hamster Society Singapore

The Hamster Society Singapore (HSS), founded by Cheryl Capelli and Chen Soong Fee, became a registered society in March 2019.

The duo, who met through a hamster interest group on Facebook, tell The Pride that poor hamster care standards in Singapore was their impetus for starting the welfare group.

Cheryl and Soong Fee from Hamster Society Singapore. *Credit: Hamster Society Singapore.*

The two were appalled that many hamster owners in Singapore were rearing hamsters the wrong way, often in direct contrast to international standards.

"Even if you've been caring for hamsters for the last 20 years the same way, it may not be the correct practice," says Soong Fee, 32, explaining why the society invests a lot of effort in education. As an official partner of Animal & Veterinary Services (AVS), it has taken part in several events to educate the public on hamster care.

It's not a one-size-fits-all solution for hamsters. The size and type of cage, bedding material and wheel size all play an important role in providing the right environment for healthy hamsters.

"You have to understand your pet as they have different needs and wants," Soong Fee says.

Hamsters that like to climb cannot be put in a bar cage, for example, even though bar cages provide more ventilation. "We've seen hamsters get broken limbs due to falling from a height in a bar cage."

Some hamsters have allergies to certain types of bedding, so owners need to watch whether their hamsters are sneezing or rubbing their noses, which are signs that dust-free bedding might be needed in order to prevent respiratory issues.

Additionally, the cages recommended by pet stores in Singapore tend to be too small, according to Soong Fee. In European countries, there are laws stipulating minimum cage sizes, and HSS hopes to advocate for similar legislation for small pets in Singapore.

Rescues and foster care forms another large part of HSS's work. The volunteers at HSS often get tip-offs of abandoned or abused hamsters via their social media channels. Often, a single rescue can bring in a large number of hamsters – usually a result of poor breeding practices.

In October 2020, HSS rescued a single batch of 129 hamsters that were kept by a suspected hoarder. Caring for the animals overwhelmed the team of more than 40 volunteer foster carers.

These foster carers form the backbone of the support that HHS gets from its volunteers.

Says Soong Fee: "When we get a big number of new hamsters, we have to ask our foster carers to take on more cases. Many of them have full-time jobs, but they find the experience rewarding."

These foster carers must be above the age of 21 and are screened stringently, in the same way potential adopters are. It's a role that requires the right mindset and commitment, as often, they would need to make many trips to the vet and give the hamsters medication.

Even though hamsters are small pets, the foster carers give their charges the best possible care. Just looking at HSS's adoption posts shows how the foster carers understand the quirks of each hamster.

Sometimes a foster carer grows to love the cuddly rescue so much that they end up adopting the hamster. "That's what we call a 'foster fail'!" Soong Fee laughs.

Small pets like hamsters are cheap to purchase, which leads to more impulse buys than other more expensive animals. There is usually an uptick in people giving up their hamsters after the long school holiday break, says Soong Fee.

"It's important to do your research before purchasing a hamster," she says.

If you think you're suited to be a pawrent, visit HSS's Adoption Gallery and get to know their latest hams waiting to be adopted!

Guinea Pig Rescue Singapore

Felicia Tan, 22, has been doing pet rescue work on and off for the past four years, caring for rabbits, hamsters, dogs, cats, as well as guinea pigs.

But in January 2021, after fostering 13 guinea pigs because their owner had suddenly died, she decided to take it to the next level by

Felicia Tan from Guinea Pig Rescue. *Credit: Felicia Tan.*

starting Guinea Pig Rescue Singapore as there was no existing group dedicated to the furry rodents.

With about 12 volunteers, most of whom are from the Proud Owners of Guinea Pigs community on Facebook, the group has rescued more than 100 guinea pigs and rehomed 44 to date.

Felicia and her team take rehoming for their rescues very seriously. She tells The Pride that in an ideal rehoming scenario, a rescued guinea pig is quarantined for two weeks and has a health check-up with a vet.

Potential adopters are screened and educated on how to make the adoption successful. For those who already own guinea pigs, a playdate is organised to see if the guinea pigs will bond, followed up with a homestay trial.

"We do reject adopters whom we find unsuitable. Occasionally, we even have to deal with some rather rude people, who just want to try their luck at getting a 'cheap' guinea pig, as our adoption fee is only $30 (which covers the cost of the vet check-up), instead of buying a guinea pig from a pet store, which can cost up to $180," Felicia explains.

Occasionally, rescued guinea pigs are taken in due to abuse or abandonment. In one particularly horrific rescue case, Felicia tells The Pride of a guinea pig they found abandoned at a lift lobby.

"He had clearly been abused – his paws were burnt black. His bandages had to be changed twice a day. The team named him

'Warrior' and he was a happy pig, but sadly, he eventually succumbed to his injuries."

In some cases, the animals require surgery and medication, and these get paid for by kind fellow guinea pig enthusiasts. Sometimes, the guinea pigs don't have a high chance of a successful surgery, so GPRS looks into long-term foster care for them as they aren't suitable for adoption.

When a guinea pig comes to GPRS in bad health, the team's priority is to address the medical issues quickly. Explains Felicia: "We don't confront the owners about why they didn't care for the pigs properly. Poor care could be due to the wrong information given by pet stores or vets who aren't familiar with guinea pig care."

"One guinea pig, Milly, was surrendered because her owners were leaving Singapore, but we discovered that she had a large ovarian cyst, a uterine infection that had gone untreated for a year, and nails so long that they curled," Felicia says.

Milly's foster carer, Anabelle, eventually adopted it even though Milly's days were numbered as its cancerous tumours could not be fully removed. "From the day I first picked her from being surrendered till now, she has brought nothing but joy and hope to me, my family and even the team," Anabelle shared on the GPRS Facebook page.

Despite all the challenges, Felicia says guinea pigs are worth the time and effort to nurture as a pet.

"Usually guinea pigs are very skittish, and run away from humans. It's quite satisfying when they grow to become comfortable with humans! When they warm up to you, they start wheeking [little squeaks], and make 'popcorns' [little jumps] and 'zoomies' [running around the cage] – it's adorable!"

Chicken Adoption Rescue Singapore

When it comes to chickens, most of us would only think of them as food, but for engineering systems design student, Noel Tan, 22, his journey as a pet chicken owner began after he became enamoured with his friend's baby chicks.

He now owns 10 chickens. And after meeting like-minded chicken enthusiasts on Facebook group Backyard Chickens Singapore, he

Noel and Simon with their pet chickens. *Credit: Chicken Adoption Rescue Singapore.*

founded Chicken Adoption Rescue Singapore (CARsg), with Simon Ong, 55, a businessman in the construction industry.

Set up in June 2020, CARsg is the first of its kind in Singapore. Its eight team members have different roles, such as building and maintaining the coop on a farm plot in Pasir Ris, caring for the chickens, and running the group's Facebook page. As the law allows rearing up to only 10 chickens on a private property, the team has had to reject chickens from people desperate to release their pets. They generally rescue ornamental birds, like Silkies and Polish chickens.

"We don't actively go out and look for wild chickens – jungle fowl have no problem surviving. It's the domestic breeds that can't survive in the wild, and need rescuing," Noel laughs.

He explains that these pets often get abandoned or surrendered after their owners, who first got the birds as cute chicks, realise that chickens can get quite noisy when fully grown.

He has come across abuse cases. In September 2020, the team was alerted to a Polish chicken abandoned in Pasir Ris Park with its legs tied up with raffia string. CARsg, which has rehomed 56 chickens successfully so far, rehabilitated the lost bird and found a new home for it.

Contrary to what you may expect, there is a demand for these rare pets and new homes are often found quite quickly, says Noel. Potential adopters are screened and the team requires them to supply photos of the home environment. No adoption fees are charged.

Silkies. *Credit: Chicken Adoption Rescue Singapore.*

Caring for the chickens. *Credit: Chicken Adoption Rescue Singapore.*

Chickens can only be kept on landed property and must have a cage or a coop as the authorities do not allow pet chickens to roam freely.

Simon, who owns 13 chickens housed in three locations, says: "Different breeds have different temperaments. Chickens are smarter than you would expect, and can be docile like a cat or dog. They can become attached to their owners too."

And in case you're wondering whether CARsg members are vegetarian, Noel says that meat (and chicken!) remains part of their diet. "No one has stopped eating chickens though some of us refrain from eating the eggs that have been laid at home!"

Couple grows community of volunteers to sew clear masks for the deaf

Face masks have made lip-reading impossible, which hampers those who rely on it to interact, especially the deaf.

by Melissa Wong

We may find wearing face masks a necessary encumbrance in the new normal, but there is a group of people in Singapore who are particularly affected by this rule – the deaf and those hard of hearing.

So married couple Oliver Guo, 33, and Amanda Chua, 31, started an initiative during the circuit breaker in May 2020 to help this group of people with a simple solution – a mask with a transparent panel.

Oliver, Amanda and Oliver's mom, Madam Cheong.
Credit: Facebook / The Simple Deed.

Called The Simple Deed, the community volunteering initiative helps to create such masks, half of which goes to The Singapore Association for the Deaf (SADeaf) every month, with the remaining half given free to the public.

Sharing a fondness for charity

The idea, while not new, is a natural progression from the couple's interest in volunteer work. Both Oliver and Amanda share a desire to give back to the community – in fact, the pair started volunteering together while they were dating.

"We wanted to look for a cause that we were both interested in. We took it as part of our dating time; an hour a week together, rather than just head to the movies," shares Oliver.

"You get to understand the people around you better and learn how to relate to different kinds of people. At the end of the day, we get to share our reflections with each other. There's really a lot of better interaction opportunities. I guess the best proof is that we are husband and wife now," he laughs.

Six years ago, they started helping out at Riding for the Disabled Association of Singapore, where horse-riding therapy sessions are provided for mentally or physically challenged people.

Then two years ago, to focus more on their immediate community, they joined a grassroots organisation in their neighbourhood and started interacting with neighbours.

Amanda tells The Pride that every month, they delivered daily necessities to lower-income families. When the circuit breaker happened, the volunteers switched to giving out vouchers instead and so had to explain to beneficiaries how to use them and where to get their groceries. That was when Oliver and Amanda realised that they had a challenge.

Identifying and overcoming the challenge

The couple realised that with their masks on, it was difficult for the elderly to understand them. This was especially challenging for those who were hard of hearing.

"It was hard to explain to them that we were giving out vouchers instead of groceries during the circuit breaker. Facial expressions and lip movements are vital for the deaf and hard-of-hearing in

Madam Cheong Yoke Fong teaching the couple to sew the masks. *Credit: Facebook / The Simple Deed.*

communication. The mask became an obstacle."

So Oliver and Amanda went online for alternatives. They found an article about the deaf community using an innovative transparent mask. Thrilled with their findings, they reached out to SADeaf and their initiative was very well received.

With no sewing experience to start with, it was Oliver who got his mum, Madam Cheong Yoke Fong, to teach them how to make a prototype. Busting out their unused sewing machines, they managed to start sewing with her guidance.

"When we first started out, my mum did most of the sewing. We had the idea, but we needed execution and action. So, it was very important that my mum helped us get started."

Oliver explains that at first, it took a more experienced seamstress like his mother an hour to make one mask – now she needs about 30 to 45 minutes. The inexperienced couple still takes an hour to sew a mask each, which is why they reached out to two friends' families who helped with quite a bit of sewing in the first phase.

As interest picked up, their pool of volunteers grew. Now, weekends for Oliver and Amanda involve less sewing and more logistical work like preparing and delivering the materials to volunteers and the finished masks to their recipients.

"We still believe firmly in the human touch, rather than being just a production factory line, so we try to meet as many of our volunteers as possible, hand delivering our materials to them. And the recipients as well, when we deliver the masks," says the couple.

"This also eases the worries of the volunteers, some of whom just want to focus on sewing without having to worry about logistics. So for now, our focus on the weekends have been working together with and complementing our volunteers – using the strength of the community, in that sense."

A community project

And help has come from the larger community as well. Some enterprises that have seen The Simple Deed's social media pages have contributed spare fabric, even allowing Oliver and Amanda to come take their pick.

Says Oliver: "We are actually very grateful to our first sponsors, CYC Made to Measure being one of them. When we first started out during the circuit breaker, materials were a lot harder to obtain. But we managed to get our first batch of fabric from CYC. Recently, we've had a lot more local tailoring companies jumping on board, such as Closeknip, Shirt Bar, Este Bartin and others."

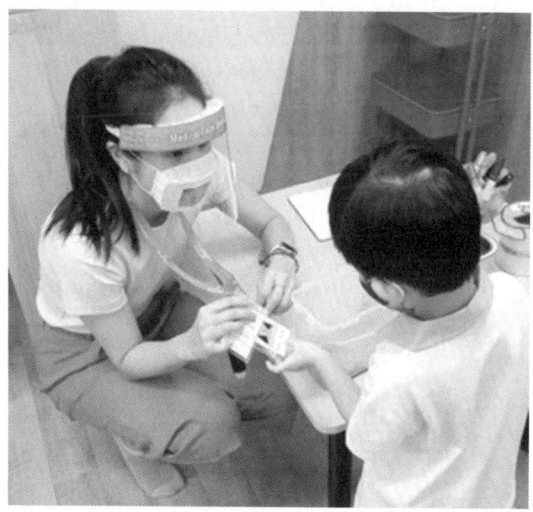

The clear face masks have allowed speech and language therapist Krystal Chng conduct speech therapy sessions more effectively.
Credit: Facebook / The Simple Deed.

Even though they have almost 30 volunteers helping with the production of the masks, other people without any sewing expertise have also stepped forward.

The couple tells The Pride: "We had a volunteer who really wanted to help out but didn't know how – he didn't have a sewing machine, nor know how to sew. He happened to have just received his motorbike license, so he helped to do a few delivery runs. It's still for the same cause and the same end goal, but he helped in a different way."

With 600 masks made and distributed so far, the initiative has far exceeded the couple's expectations. "We were only looking at making a hundred masks at first, but we've surprisingly had such a great response from the community," they say.

It's a humbling and encouraging experience, say Oliver and Amanda. They have had preschool teachers, parents with young children, speech therapists and many people from different walks of life ask for the clear masks. One of the preschools even got the kids to do an artwork in appreciation!

Some bumps on the road

Of course it wasn't smooth sailing all the way.

"We are limited to the volunteers' free time. Now in Phase 2, kids have exams and need to be cared for, and people are going back to work. We used to have more active volunteers, but they can't produce as much as before. Some also, after receiving the materials, have realised that it's a lot more challenging than it seems from videos and guides," the couple shares.

And it is important for Oliver and Amanda that people are truly happy volunteering. Now that most are back to the grind and have less free time on their hands, the pair want to ensure that there is no pressure to deliver.

They explain: "It's not a factory line. We could have easily gone commercial and reached out to commercial partners, but we wanted it to be a community volunteering initiative."

The couple also hopes to do some research and development to produce more comfortable, better-fitting and well-protected masks, to encourage more people, not just the hard-of-hearing, to wear clear masks.

"It will help the society be more inclusive because if the ones around those hard-of-hearing wear it, it actually really benefits them," says Oliver.

"SADeaf alone has more than 6,000 members. If we distribute two masks to each household, that's already 12,000 masks required. And we've only made 600 so far, so we are really far away from our goal. If we want to encourage all of Singapore to put on the mask it is such a tough call."

Making the mask more aesthetically pleasing remains part of the dream. When they first started, the masks received considerable pushback from people: one common feedback was that the mask appears scary because it makes the mouth look exposed.

Amanda explains: "It's not widely adopted yet, so some people still feel like the minority when they wear it. We've only made 600 in all of Singapore, so those wearing it may get strange stares."

Documenting their journey

When Oliver and Amanda found out that the National Library Board was launching a campaign called Documenting COVID-19 in Singapore, asking for the public to submit stories of what they've been doing during circuit breaker, they thought it would be the perfect opportunity to document their initiative and the process of them learning to sew.

"To us, it started off really being like a diary, wanting to document what we were doing during the circuit breaker. But it became much more than that. And we're very glad our initiative has benefitted those in the community," the couple says.

If there is one thing Oliver and Amanda want to inspire in Singaporeans, it is to volunteer to a cause through a method that you prefer. There is no one fixed way to contribute your time and effort.

"There are so many volunteering opportunities within our community. It's hard to keep up with the motivation with volunteering, so it's important to do something you believe in and enjoy."

These special needs dancers set the stage for more inclusivity and diversity

Despite their disabilities, dancers from DADC are empowered to take on leadership roles and give back to the community.

by Serene Leong

"Dancing with masks is really not easy!" Subastian Tan exclaims as he takes a short break.

It is a Thursday afternoon and the 25-year-old dance trainer is in a studio with three other dancers preparing for a performance for Children's Day.

They listen attentively to Subastian and follow his lead, creating Bharatanatyam-inspired hand movements as they move gracefully around the room.

There is something different about these dancers though.

Some of the dancers from DADC. *Credit: Facebook / DADC.*

Most of them are from the Diverse Abilities Dance Collective (DADC) and have Down syndrome. Subastian, the programme leader, hopes to provide a platform for their stories to be shared with others.

Since Singapore's Phase 2 reopening, these special dancers have started to meet for weekly studio rehearsals again, keeping to a reduced group size of five.

DADC, a division of Maya Dance Theatre (MDT), was started in 2018 to provide semi-professional dance opportunities for people of all abilities. It is a community initiative by the company to create a co-existing space for persons with disabilities and art-makers.

Sharing lived experiences

Subastian, who recently graduated from Singapore Management University (SMU), works as a full-time project artist with MDT. He tells The Pride that he sees the special-needs dancers he works with no differently from any other performer.

He says: "When we tap on the perspectives, stories and backgrounds of each person, we get to see them holistically and that comes out through their dance, their art, their music.

"We want people to recognise that everyone is unique, and we have our own set of lived experiences and all of that is useful and worthy to be shared."

For example, one member, June Lin, 36, recently created a solo dance piece in which she uses a chair as a prop to represent her older brother, who works long hours, to show her love for him.

June performing her solo piece. *Credit: Facebook / DADC.*

As programme leader, Subastian manages the team of 15 dancers and trainers, planning dance training sessions and workshops, as well as teaching them other employable skills like administration or wardrobe management.

Four of the DADC dancers are already working part time at Apsara Asia, an arts education social enterprise.

Dancing isn't just a way of finding employment or expression, it enables the dancers to exercise. Being able to utilise different parts of their bodies increases their physical fitness as well as improves their confidence and self-esteem.

And Subastian says that it is the little details, the small victories that keeps him inspired to continue working with the group.

He says: "One of our members used to keep her hands clenched tightly. It's partly physical and partly neurological. Along the way, as she has been training with us through dance, she has learnt to open up her hands."

Adapting to Covid-19

Right now, the dancers are rehearsing for Mighty Mousedeer Of The Forest. In the performance, each dancer takes on the character of a different animal.

Initially, the production was planned to be a live performance as part of the Arts in Your Neighbourhood programme spearheaded by the National Arts Council. But due to safe distancing measures, the live performance has been cancelled and DADC will be adapting the piece into a video recording, to be live-streamed for children and their families on Children's Day.

"There's a bit of Indian dance nuance to it, so there might be some fun to play with the hand gestures," Subastian says, explaining that during the post-show activity, dancers will share some of the dance movements.

"More importantly, because we are sharing the stage with persons with disabilities, I hope that children from a young age will get to see that they might be different, but we can still coexist, we can play with each other, dance with each other. And there's nothing that's stopping us from doing that."

Adjusting to the changes caused by Covid-19 has not been easy for the team especially when live rehearsals were out of the question

Subastian (far left) leading a rehearsal for Mighty Mousedeer Of The Forest. *Credit: Serene Leong.*

and they had to work on Zoom during the circuit breaker. Subastian says that he needed to come up with new ways to train and rehearse.

He adds: "Instead of exploring movements, we were talking a lot more about how the characters are feeling and responding. We were observing each other a lot more as well, because we can't all dance at the same time. It's taken a slightly slower pace, but it's allowed us to go deeper into our practice.

"The dancers have a lot of passion and drive. Ultimately, the discipline to train still has to come from them, whether online or in the studio, as things keep changing."

Giving back to the community

Despite not being able to meet, DADC took the initiative during the circuit breaker to give back to the community. The team facilitated and recorded simple hand and body exercises to be shared with the elderly in nursing homes and senior activity centres to keep them physically active.

Subastian says: "As much as we are receiving support in our programmes, we want to give back as well and we encourage the dancers to contribute in their own way. That's why we thought of this movement programme to share what we do best – dance."

While he is the programme leader, Subastian says that he gives his dancers chances to take the reins. This can come in small things, like leading the warm-up sessions during training, to bigger responsibilities, like co-training a class of students.

Arassi (left) and Subastian (centre) conducting a children's class at The Artground. *Credit: Facebook / DADC.*

"Whenever there are opportunities, it's important for us to guide them into these roles so that society can normalise seeing persons with disabilities in leadership roles," he says.

It is visible from the way the team interacts that DADC is very much a family. Subustian shares that it warms his heart to see how everyone looks out for each other. As he is usually busy with many activities, one member, Arassi Rajkumar, 27, who affectionately calls him "Sub", often reminds the team to take a break.

"She might buy a small snack and leave it in the office and say, 'remember to eat ah'. Each of them shows their love in different ways to each other," he adds.

The DADC dancers have hopes and dreams too. For example, another member, Chen Wanyi, 31, who works part-time with Apsara Asia and has a housekeeping job at a hotel on Sentosa, tells The Pride that she hopes to work in the fashion and music industry.

"It's hard for me to stay focused on one thing. I prefer to take it slow, step by step. Once I reach my goal I can reward myself, give myself a treat, and treat my DADC family to enjoy the moment and have fun," Wanyi says.

She adds: "They make me happy. I like to laugh with them, smile with them. They inspire me… We learn together and they also teach me. We really get along with each other and we just like having a conversation together."

Inclusive café prepares meals for low-income families with special needs children

Special needs school starts donation drive to help feed needy families struggling to provide daily meals for children.

by Mirta Syazanna

For the majority of us living in Singapore, food is never scarce, even when our movements were restricted during the circuit breaker. Breakfast, lunch or dinner could be easily ordered and delivered to our doorstep with just a few taps on our phone.

In the past week alone, most of us would have eaten various dishes and cuisines readily available in our cosmopolitan city.

But for some low-income families, their three daily meals consist of only rice and sardines.

This is the reality that My Inspiring Journey (MIJ) Special Education Hub found when speaking to some of the students under its Financial Assistance Scheme.

Volunteers delivering food to low-income families. *Credit: MIJ Hub.*

Established in 2011, MIJ is a school for students with special needs such as autism, attention deficit hyperactivity disorder (ADHD), Down syndrome, dyslexia and global developmental delay (GDD). The one-stop centre of about 300 students provides school readiness, care for youth as well as intervention programmes for individuals with special needs from ages four to 30.

MIJ's husband-and-wife founders, Mohammad Ali Dawood and Faraliza Zainal, set up the school for their son, Mohd Ashraf, who has autism and tuberous sclerosis.

Mohammad Ali Dawood and Faraliza Zainal with their son Mohd Ashraf. *Credit: MIJ Hub.*

As part of MIJ's engagement efforts with its students, it made calls to families to find out how they were coping after the circuit breaker. It was from these check-ins that they realised that many lower-income parents were struggling to provide proper meals for their family.

Nasrul Rohmat, MIJ's business development manager says: "It was greatly disheartening to hear the pain they were going through in their everyday lives.

"The families shared that they ate the same food for breakfast, lunch and dinner. Most of the time, they could only have rice, egg and soy sauce for their family."

After a discussion, the team at MIJ decided to initiate The Takeout Campaign.

Beneficiaries grateful for extra help

So far, MIJ has been reaching out to families with meals prepared at its in-house special-needs café called Ashraf's Cafe.

Poster for The Takeout Campaign (left). Ashraf delivering food to one of the beneficiaries (right). Credit: MIJ Hub.

And the recipients have been thankful for the extra help provided, Nasrul tells The Pride.

"The Takeout Campaign helps lighten not only the family's monthly expenses but also their workload. It is already undeniably tough to take care of children with special needs, what more juggling household matters," he says.

One such beneficiary is ten-year-old Mardhiyyah.

Mardhiyyah was born with a genetic hearing impairment and lost her hearing as she got older. She started using hearing aids when she was three and had her first cochlear implant when she was six years old.

This month, she will be getting her second implant, this time in her right ear. But even with the most powerful hearing aids, it will still be difficult for her to hear.

Due to her condition, Mardhiyyah's mother stopped working to care for her. Her 69-year-old father recently started a job as a cleaner. He hadn't worked for a year due to health complications. When he was ill, the family had difficulty paying their bills. There were times when they did not even have basic toiletries, such as shampoo, at home. They also had to stop Mardhiyyah's lessons at MIJ. However, Mardhiyyah's situation recently improved when her aunt stepped in to pay the monthly school fees.

Food is usually limited in Mardhiyyah's household. Most days, they eat instant noodles, fishball soup or rice and egg for dinner. At times, there is no food for lunch.

The Takeout Campaign has helped to alleviate some of their day-to-day struggles.

"I hope for this campaign to continue to run for as long as possible. Even if it does not, we are very grateful for everything," Mardhiyyah tells The Pride.

Similarly, 18-year-old Qisthi Isyraqi is also appreciative of the initiative. Qisthi, who has autism, attends ASPN Delta Senior School – which offers vocational training to students with mild intellectual disability – and lives in a two-room rental flat with his 56-year-old grandmother. She is his main caregiver.

Qisthi's father passed away when he was two years old and he has lived with his grandmother since. His mother lives separately with his younger brother. They do not meet regularly, only during Hari Raya, due to Qisthi's aggression and anxiety issues.

He has been attending lessons every weekend at MIJ since 2017.

"I am very grateful for this initiative. My grandmother and I are unable to afford delicious food. When we receive food from MIJ and Ashraf's Cafe, we get to taste something different than our usual meal," shares Qisthi.

Providing hot, fresh meals for needy families

Ashraf's Cafe is an inclusive café set up by MIJ. The café creates a safe space to help special-needs individuals get used to working in a real-life job environment.

Mohammad Ali Dawood and Faraliza Zainal's 20-year-old son Ashraf works at the café that bears his name. He tells The Pride: "Although I have autism, I am able to help others and my friends

Credit: MIJ Hub.

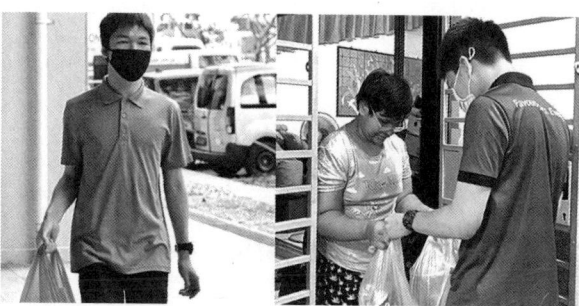

Credit: MIJ Hub.

who are in need. It makes me feel confident and happy. I want to make my parents and job coaches proud of me."

Meals for The Takeout Campaign are prepared at Ashraf's Cafe. Every meal is made around noon to ensure that its beneficiaries can receive fresh, warm food in the evening.

When asked how he feels about meeting the families when delivering the food, Ashraf says: "I am always excited when I meet the families. They are all very friendly. When the parents tap my shoulder and say thank you, I sometimes laugh uncontrollably because I feel shy. I want to continue to meet them and give them delicious food prepared by my colleagues and me."

Nasrul explains that the initiative not only provides meals for low-income families but also gives the special-needs employees of Ashraf's Cafe greater work fulfillment. The menu and ingredients are also selected with extra care – everything is made with healthy and fresh ingredients and is special-needs friendly.

More awareness needed

MIJ has set up a donation page for The Takeout Campaign and while response has been good so far, more funds are needed for MIJ to help even more lower-income families with special-needs children.

Right now, MIJ distributes one meal once a week but hopes to be able to cater meals to its beneficiaries up to three times a week.

"I hope that more people can donate to The Takeout Campaign so that more of my friends and their families who cannot afford to eat at cafés or restaurants, can enjoy better food in their own homes," says Ashraf.

He gives old books and young children a second chance at life

Singaporean sells second-hand books
to help children and youth in some of the world's
most isolated communities get an education.

by Serene Leong

When Singaporean Randall Chong went on a solo backpacking trip to Nepal in December 2017, he did not expect that he would make seven trips back to the country in the next two years, let alone quit his job to raise money full-time for children's education.

Today, the 28-year-old founder of social enterprise Books Beyond Borders (BBB) collects and sells quality second-hand books to fund educational projects in rural Nepal.

His goal? For every child to have access to education.

Randall runs Books Beyond Borders single-handedly, and apart from a student intern who helps with the online bookstore, does everything himself – he built his website, handles the social media and

Randall interacting with the children in Nepal. *Credit: Randall Chong.*

even packs the books for sale (from a spare room in his grandfather's home).

He also commits 100% of all donations and profits from book sales to fund educational causes.

Randall tells The Pride: "I love what I do. I love reading. I have an entire shelf of books on global poverty. And I'm building my own business. It's a great start for me."

"I'm also passionate and committed to the people and communities that I've met in Nepal... If I can make use of my skills to create a sustainable impact for all these people, it's exciting."

Doing one thing that scares him

"During the first week, I would walk eight hours alone each day. I got lost so many times. There was no one on the trek because it was during the coldest season."

But on day seven or eight, Randall says that he noticed a boy trailing him and decided to approach him. Even though they barely understood each other, and used gestures to communicate awkwardly, he found out that he was a local porter who was transporting goods on his back from one village to another. His name was Madan and he was only 16.

Randall soon discovered that it was not uncommon for children and youths in the villages to be out of school and working instead.

He says: "I became curious, 'Why are kids like Madan not in school? Where do these people go to school?' For the rest of the trek, my perspective changed. It was no longer about the mountains. I

Walking eight hours a day in Nepal. *Credit: Randall Chong.*

started to notice things and ask questions. 'Why are all the mothers so young, why are the women in the field, why are all the young boys working as porters? I wanted to visit a school. I was interested to see what a school looked like.'"

A month later, he got the opportunity when a local Nepalese man invited him to visit a local primary school, a ten-hour drive into the mountains near Tibet.

"When I got there, I understood why youths like Madan drop out or are not interested in school. The school had no resources. The classroom had blank walls, teachers didn't turn up for classes, and the students simply had nothing to read at all," Randall says.

"I felt pretty helpless. I didn't know what I could offer. I sat [in one of the classrooms] for 30 minutes, took some photos and left."

"I had two options. I could ask them what they needed, go back to Singapore, raise some money, bring some friends to paint some walls, and then go back to my day job. Or I could start an organisation that could support all these people at the bottom of the pyramid, and do so in a way that is long term."

He chose the latter.

Having zero experience in the non-profit sector, Randall says that the scariest thing he did in Nepal was not scaling Mount Everest base camp on his own, but taking the leap to quit his job and start Books Beyond Borders in 2018.

Primary school kids reading the only thing available to them in the classroom. *Credit: Randall Chong.*

Students with the donated school bags and books. *Credit: Facebook / Books Beyond Borders.*

Changing lives one book at a time

700 Backpacks in 7 Days was the first project Books Beyond Borders funded. Working with Rotaract clubs in Nepal, Randall distributed 669 school bags and books to needy students in six schools.

Randall says: "In seven days, we raised over US$10,000 and mobilised more than 20 local volunteers with our partners to reach the goal."

In an effort to understand how resource-starved communities can move out of the poverty cycle, Randall says he visited dozens of remote villages across Nepal to meet with local leaders and teachers in the community.

He says: "Many people think it's a resource issue in these underdeveloped countries, that once we raise money, we can solve the problem. But it's much deeper than that. Poverty is a very complex issue. It's not something that money can solve. There's a lot of politics involved."

"That's why I spend a lot of time learning, speaking with government officials, finding out from our partners what's working and what's not, and what is the best way that we can run projects to create the most impact."

This is also one of the reasons why Books Beyond Borders doesn't send books to Nepal, but instead works with domestic publishers to support the country's economy to produce children's books written by local authors in the Nepalese language.

Randall also speaks to the students to find out their perspective.

He recalls: "At a school in one of the poorest villages I visited, I asked the students, 'If you could have anything for the school, what would it be?' There were the usual answers of 'a volleyball', 'a lamp'. Then, there was this Grade 8 student [equivalent to Secondary 2], Dham, who said he wanted a first-aid kit and a bicycle pump. And I got really curious."

"We visited Dham at his home and I spoke to him and his family. The community that he lives in is very poor. He said a lot of students are not going to school because they get hurt playing sports so he thought a first-aid kit could solve the problem and I was really touched by that. He also wanted a bicycle pump because kids like him walk two hours to get to school, and most of the tyres on their bikes are flat."

Randall says: "All these small problems that cause students not to go to school can actually be solved easily. Some of the solutions are not expensive if you just take the time to speak to these people and understand the real problem."

He says that many of the students he interacts with are really hardworking and have the potential to succeed.

To Randall, the importance of having an education is more than just obtaining a certificate. It brings dignity and confidence, especially to the youth in developing countries like Nepal, he says.

Through Books Beyond Borders, Randall helped fund the first school library in Lahara. The western Nepalese village is one of the most isolated communities in the world.
Credit: Facebook / Books Beyond Borders.

Randall and his translator (second from right) speaking with Dham (second from left) and his father (far right) in their home. *Credit: Randall Chong.*

"The way people treat you and look at you is different. It's a big deciding factor whether you make it in life."

He explains that in Nepal, education is crucial because the longer the children stay in school, the later they have to face life in the outside world. Without education, girls are married off in their teens and boys get sent overseas, often to Gulf countries, where they work in dangerous conditions.

Randall claims that every day, deaths from these dangerous jobs go unreported. Bodies are being sent back to Nepalese families and there's also a high potential for trafficking.

He says: "Besides literacy, education can stop all these real problems in the world, and that's what I'm very passionate about."

Making a sustainable impact

When Covid-19 hit, schools in Nepal were shut down and Books Beyond Borders had to adapt. It co-funded an audio teaching project with Teach For Nepal where teachers could record their lessons for radio stations to broadcast to students in the villages that did not have access to the Internet.

Last month, Books Beyond Borders also funded 2,000 workbooks designed by teachers for home-based learning.

Unfortunately, despite Randall's best efforts, Covid-19 has undone some of the progress Books Beyond Borders has made in Nepal.

Randall chatting with the Nepalese students. *Credit: Facebook / Books Beyond Borders.*

Randall says that he has had to stop several projects due to school closures. Recently though, schools have been gradually reopening, albeit intermittently for a few weeks at a time.

He says: "Based on research done by our partners during this period, many students have quit school permanently, and it's quite troubling."

However, he does see a silver lining in the Covid crisis. Books Beyond Borders is receiving and selling more books.

"People have more time at home, they read more. People also declutter more so I get more books!"

He has also modified his business model. At first, he relied mostly on donations and fundraising from friends and willing donors. Now, with a focus more on collecting and selling books to generate profits for fundraising, Books Beyond Borders is more sustainable and less reliant on the economy and external factors, explains Randall.

"For the first time this year I got a salary!" he says, adding that it was a boost of confidence for him as he didn't receive any pay for the first year and a half when the business operated on a charitable model.

Books Beyond Borders also launched its online bookstore in March 2020. Since then, it has funded three projects with Teach For Nepal without soliciting any donations from the public.

Randall's dream for Books Beyond Borders is to become as big as international online bookstore Book Depository, but for quality second-hand books.

"If we can get to that capacity, we can generate more money to fund more projects, and I can expand my impact not just in Nepal, but in other countries around the world."

He admits that he is very lucky to have the support of his friends and family.

He says: "My mum helps me to pack books at night, and taught me how to wrap them nicely. My parents never question what I do. They never fully understand, but they know I'm doing good, so they are glad."

And Randall expresses his gratitude through a personal handwritten note thanking each customer.

Randall shares that in the past, he used to think that the best measure of accomplishment was monetary wealth. But his path over the past few years had shown him that real value comes from investing in the well-being of others.

He says: "There are days I fall into a rut when I look at what other people are doing and their success… but I've learnt that we are all chasing different things, and to me that's okay. I just want to focus on my own thing and not let what other people are doing distract me."

And spending time with the students in Nepal have also reinforced this lesson for him. "They all have their own goal and aspirations. It may not be as lofty as some of ours but if they can achieve that, they are happy."

Books Beyond Borders funded 2,000 workbooks to be distributed to students who were struggling to study without the Internet during Covid-19. *Credit: Randall Chong.*

She sets up online business to help single mums remember how strong they are

Entrepreneur sets up online business to help single mums get extra income through baked goodies.

by Mirta Syazanna

Like many mums of young children, Suzlina Rahman's day starts at 5.30am.

What's different is that after she sends off her two children, aged 11 and four, to school, she cracks open her laptop to check emails and clear the week's events with her team of bakers and deliverymen.

Suzlina, 39, is the founder of Curated by Suz, a small home business selling cookies and cakes made by single and stay-at-home mothers, helping them market their baked goods to the wider

(From left) Yannie, Suzlina and Lynn. *Credit: Suzlina Rahman.*

community. This arrangement provides an additional supplement to the bakers' main source of income as they receive up to 80% of the profits made through the platform.

Suzlina tells The Pride: "After I left my full-time position in 2015, I volunteered with an association that helps domestic abuse victims. From this experience, I realised how strong this group of women were and the sacrifices they made for their children. Also, they had built their own support system in the shelters. They helped to care for each other's kids when it became too overwhelming for the mothers. It made me think of ways I could help this group of women to move forward and for them to feel their worth, because along the way they forget how valued they are to society.

"I think that this is the same feeling for any mother out there, regardless of whether you are a domestic abuse victim or not. We tend to forget how much we are worth as we get too caught up with our multiple roles," she adds.

So when an acquaintance who owned a boutique selling *baju kurung* wanted to venture into selling cookies as wedding favours in 2019, Suzlina realised that this was an opportunity to start a business to engage mothers as home bakers, as she knew there were many talented ones out there.

One of them is 40-year-old Lynn Hamid, a single mother with a 17-year-old son. Suzlina approached her and she became Curated by Suz's first official home baker.

Single mum turns hobby into earnings

Lynn became a single mother at the young age of 23. She started baking as a hobby in 2007 after she attended free classes for single mothers provided by the Singapore Muslim Women's Association.

The programme allowed single mothers like Lynn to earn extra income by baking and selling cookies every Hari Raya. Soon after, Lynn, who specialises in chocolate chip cookies and Nutella tarts, started baking for family and friends and also packing her cookies in small party packs.

Curated by Suz has helped Lynn, who has no knowledge of marketing, reach out to a wider audience instead of relying on the support of just family and friends.

Lynn with a selection of the items she has baked.
Credit: Suzlina Rahman.

"By working together with Suzlina, it grew my business and I am happy to know that my hobby has turned into a business and is generating income for me," says Lynn.

Single mum juggles work, kids and baking

For Yannie, 39, who has two children aged 12 and 10 years old, Curated by Suz has allowed her to continue improving herself for their sake.

For the past seven years, Yannie has had to do most things alone, including taking care of her children's needs such as their finances, education, emotional and physical well-being.

Yannie shares: "I have no other people to help with my finances so I had to work full-time and depend on myself to ensure my family's needs are taken care of. This made me stronger and independent."

Working with Suzlina provides Yannie the additional income to supplement her family's needs. As a sales executive, she juggles her time between the kids and baking – spending weekends with the children, and baking in the night after she returns home from work.

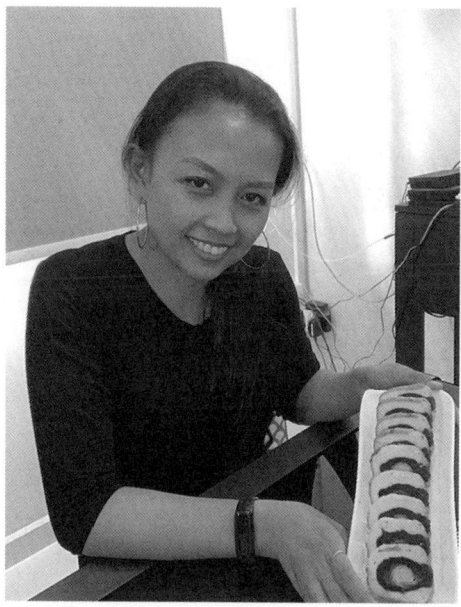

Yannie has managed to supplement her family's finances by selling her baked goods. *Credit: Suzlina Rahman.*

"I also get to hone my baking skills as I like to bake. The feedback provided by customers helps me to improve to produce tastier treats for them." she adds.

"I don't employ them, it's a partnership"

The bakers from Curated by Suz have the necessary certifications to bake at home and they already have their own small group of customers. However, what they lacked was the marketing and development know-how to grow their businesses.

That is where Suzlina fills the gap. She tells The Pride that Curated by Suz helps to promote and market the baked goods to its own pool of customers and is continuously developing partnerships with selected businesses as a supplier of cookies, cakes and tarts.

"We seek partnerships and possible collaborations to create a win-win situation for our bakers and our partners. We also handle queries from customers. We do participate in food fairs as a team."

But it's not just a business for her. It is a community partnership that she envisions.

A selection of items for sale. *Credit: Instagram / Curated by Suz.*

"We do not employ these mothers to bake for us as I see it as a partnership with these mothers. We support each other in our respective areas of strength in order to build this business," Suzlina tells The Pride.

She says the business model has had positive feedback from the public.

"Singaporeans are very generous people and I think it is in our upbringing to help others in times of need. We have a customer as young as 17 who travelled from Woodlands to the east to collect tarts she ordered just to support our single mother bakers," she shares with a smile.

During the circuit breaker, Suzlina had to put a pause to the business due to the Covid-19 clampdown on home-based businesses.

When Phase 2 kicked in, she immediately put things back into motion and launched a new product – Yannie's *tapak kuda* or horseshoe roll cake. As workers have started to return to the office, Suzlina says she has had requests for deliveries as a welcome back gift or to cheer someone up who was still working from home.

Suzlina also resumed discussions with corporate event partners, who have been similarly affected by the pandemic. As fellow entrepreneurs, they motivate one another to keep going.

"Sales can never be the same as last year. The world has come to a standstill and we can never go back to how it was pre-Covid but we have to make the best of what we have now and keep on working hard," she says.

Running the business alone is not easy for Suzlina and while she gets a lot of encouragement from her single-mum partners, it is her children that inspire her to keep going when she doubts herself.

"I talk to my 11-year-old daughter frequently about my work and in one of our conversations I was talking about the longevity of my business. She asked me to continue what I am doing and not stop because one day she would like to continue my work too.

"Many times we have no idea the things we do have an indirect impact on others. When I heard what my daughter said, I was reminded that my purpose is to help others. It serves as a testament that what I am doing has a positive impact on her life too," Suzlina shares.

Suzlina plans to increase the variety of products in Curated by Suz and partner with more single-mum bakers.

Although she works with bakers whom she already knows and trusts, Suzlina is keen to find other women who would be a good fit for the business. She also hopes to partner with organisations that believe in her cause to grow the business so that she can continue helping these mothers.

Suzlina says: "I would like to be able to give hope and encouragement to this strong group of women and for them to feel appreciated for their talents."

Appreciating our migrant workers

A learning journey showed me the harsh realities migrant workers face every day

Stepping into the shoes of the migrant worker community has helped me to see that our worlds are not that different after all. Where they intersect, opportunities of kindness appear.

by Serene Leong

It is February 2020. We are in Bangla Square at Syed Alwi Road in Little India, the meeting place for Singapore's almost 200,000 Bangladeshi migrant workers. This is where the migrant community gathers to mingle with family and friends on evenings and days off. This is their home away from home.

Surrounding Bangla Square are minimarts selling vegetables and daily necessities, coffee shops, Internet cafés, hotels, money changers and, incongruously, two rows of portable toilets. This social space, just a stone's throw away from the lights of Mustafa Centre, has everything to serve the needs of the migrant community.

Shops in the area stock items for the migrant community.

A condominium showroom not far from Bangla Square.

Standing here feels like stepping into a different world. I am aware of how out of place we look – a group of ten Chinese 20-somethings winding through human traffic, peering inquisitively into shops we normally would not find ourselves in.

That was in February.

It is April now when I write this. It is a different world now, in a totally different way. The world has turned on its head. Covid overshadows everything.

Last night (April 6), I visited Bangla Square again. The day before Singapore ordered non-essential services closed. Bangla Square is still bustling, but there is a tension in the air. Perhaps it is a reaction to the three Covid-19 clusters that have sprung up in workers' dormitories over the weekend, or the fact that Mustafa is shut for two weeks after a cluster emerged there on April 2.

Back in February, the tension I feel is that of an outsider; the migrant men stare curiously at us as we approach. I feel as though we are invading their space.

Two streets away from Bangla Square, next to City Square Mall, Peranakan shophouses are being listed for $4.6 million. At least three condominiums tower over the mall and there is a showroom for an upcoming building project.

There is a stark contrast between Bangla Square and its nearby upmarket establishments – a juxtaposition between the have and have-nots, familiar and unfamiliar, permanent and transient.

You might wonder why I ramble. This is not a typical conversation I would have with a friend.

I admit I had always perceived migrant workers as a generalised 'other'. Sure, they build our homes. I see them as I go about my day – at construction sites, repairing MRT escalators, or resting in void decks. I read about them in the news – when the Little India riots were plastered on the front pages of newspapers in 2013, and more recently, the Covid-19 clusters that emerged from several dormitories and construction sites, resulting in the quarantine of 20,000 workers.

But they occupy a separate reality that is disparate from mine.

In February, however, I am on a learning journey organised by Migrant x Me, a social enterprise that provides public education on the migrant worker community in Singapore, and I am here "to understand", as I tell our group facilitators.

Volunteer facilitators, Victoria, 29, and Guangci, 21, encourage us to "dig deeper into the surface and to have a second thought why there is prejudice or why you might even be prejudiced."

"We make quick assumptions when we don't know about something. It's part of our human psyche," Victoria says.

Where there are NGOs that support and directly assist the migrant workers, including Humanitarian Organisation for Migration Economics (HOME), Transient Workers Count Too (TWC2) and HealthServe, Migrant x Me reaches out mainly to Singaporeans and focuses on public education.

"For the past five or six years, when I was in the scene, there was no one doing [public education] and I saw that it was a need because public awareness is still low," says Isabel Phua, 25, founder of Migrant x Me.

Facilitator Guangci (right) conducting the walking tour during the Migrant x Me Learning Journey.

One of many signs around Bangla Square.

"An IPS (Institute of Policy Studies) survey showed that youths are still not as open to migrants because of lack of interaction and understanding. So I see ourselves as that platform to bridge that," she adds.

It had never occured to me before why migrant workers seemed to be on their phones all the time, though I did question how they could afford a phone with their $500 salaries, not taking into account hefty agent fees that could go as high as $20,000.

The answer is simple. Connection.

"It is a luxury for them to go back [to their home country] as they may not have the time and money," Victoria says. "Kids have to get used to growing up seeing their father on screens."

Migrant workers return home to their families only once every few years. Putting myself in their shoes, I too would be willing to purchase a phone just to hear my loved ones, even if it put me in debt.

It's easy to take something like family and friends for granted when we stay in such close proximity to them.

"Companionship is something to think about. We don't think about it because we have friends, but they don't," says SMU undergraduate Lee Wai, 22.

The volunteers, who strike up conversations with the migrant workers occasionally, share that most can speak some English.

"Some are passionate about sports, some talk about their families, and even girlfriends in Singapore," Guangci says. "When both parties are trying, you can always have a conversation."

Although I am heartened that the government and NGOs have stepped in to support the migrant worker community by providing

Participants of the Migrant x Me Learning Journey listening to the facilitators during an earlier programme. *Credit: Migrant x Me.*

amenities such as polyclinics and soup kitchens, their needs go beyond the physical.

Are the minimarts, Internet cafés and curry houses along Bangla Square really enough to meet the needs of the migrant workers?

Migrant workers are humans who deserve kindness and dignity too. They crave companionship just like us.

At the end of the night, the ten of us disperse. I return home to the comfort of my four-room flat in Bukit Batok and the luxury of a hot shower.

The next day, I pen a simple thank-you card and give it to a migrant worker in my neighbourhood.

In light of the Covid-19 outbreak in the workers' dormitories, I reach out to Isabel again who shared that the cases of infected workers has unfortunately exacerbated xenophobic sentiments among the public.

"People are shunning foreign workers because they think they are infected [with the coronavirus]," Isabel says.

"The situation in the dormitories was a ticking time bomb and this outbreak definitely highlights the importance of having dormitories that are with proper sanitation."

Stepping into the shoes of the migrant worker community has helped me to see that our worlds are not that different after all. Where they intersect, opportunities for kindness appear.

I remember what Guangci told me during our visit to Bangla Square: "Not everyone can go on a learning journey, but you can be their learning journey."

My learning journey has just begun.

He searches for foreign workers in forgotten dorms

As the country grappled with the early stages of the pandemic, one Singaporean goes on a lonely journey to help those left behind.

by Solomon Lim

Every day since the start of April, he has been exploring the nooks and crannies in Tuas, looking for small factory-converted dorms (FCDs) where migrant workers have been cooped up since the Covid-19 outbreak in the foreign worker dormitories broke out.

In the past week alone, Samuel Lim, a volunteer with the Hope Initiative Alliance (HIA), has found and reached out to eight such dorms, which house almost 1,000 workers in total.

He tells The Pride in an exclusive interview about the challenges facing these migrant workers.

"These guys are cooped up, 12 to 24 in a room, 24 hours a day. Food is one of the few things they can look forward to."

One of the workers receiving food from behind a fence. *Credit: Samuel Lim.*

Samuel delivers fruits and snacks to workers at the dorms. He also goes out at 3am to deliver Ramadan meals. *Credit: Samuel Lim.*

Samuel says that the workers, who are mostly from India and Bangladesh and work in a mix of industries ranging from marine to construction, told him that they have not had enough food to eat and have had to dig into their own pockets to get proper meals.

He says that they told him that government funds had been allocated to the companies but they have not been adequately supplied with food. This led him to start a fund-raiser with his church to help feed these men. So far, Samuel says, they have raised $15,000 and he hopes that this amount will help him feed workers for the next six weeks or so.

He shared about how he started on his personal project.

"Searching for FCDs was what I started with [before the lockdown], but after being on the ground and meeting the guys, you get to know them. I was literally knocking on doors, searching car parks, abandoned buildings and found a couple [of these dorms]. Now that I'm connected with the workers, many of them have become my friends, they send me the information through text and that's how I've located the bulk of the FCDs."

The larger dorms have had a lot of attention from the media and government agencies already and so Samuel wants to help find the smaller dorms that may have fallen through the cracks.

Samuel, whose job in advertising allows him the flexibility of volunteering his time during the circuit breaker, has been going out under the auspices of HIA to identify such dorms. When he finds these dorms, he reports them to HIA, which would then provide these workers with two meals a day. On a daily basis, HIA provides up to 24,000 meals to foreign workers in dormitories across Singapore.

In his personal capacity and with the funds raised by his church, Samuel also supplements these meals with fruits and snacks. In the past week, he tells The Pride, he has delivered 8,885 fruits that he sourced from a local supplier.

Speaking to the 31-year-old, it is easy to see the passion that he has for his work.

"I'm in touch with [the workers], and it is an extremely trying situation. Many of them maintain happy faces when speaking to their families back home. They know in their hearts of the danger they're in, but they don't show it when they call home because they don't want their families to worry."

And it is a worrisome time for them, and for Singapore.

Since the outbreak in the foreign worker dorms, the world has watched in concern as Singapore has raced to try to stay ahead of the problem. In the weeks since, volunteers and healthcare personnel have worked tirelessly to battle the virus in the dorms.

While there may be room for legitimate discussion on the inherent living conditions that our migrant workers face in Singapore, there is time for that after dealing with the issues at hand – which is the health, safety and welfare of these men now.

Samuel understands that and says he is not focused on the negative. "It's an incredibly complex problem – companies, too, are suffering as all work has halted. You can't completely point your finger at anyone to blame. What I've seen is an overflow of compassion, people doing what they can, where they are, with what they have.

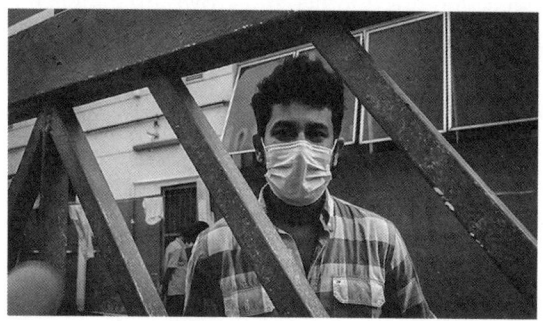

Sejal Alamin, from Bangladesh, is one of the foreign workers that Samuel has befriended. *Credit: Samuel Lim.*

Samuel shares the work he does as a volunteer with his church in regular updates. *Credit: Samuel Lim.*

That has been immensely encouraging, seeing our island united against adversity, standing in and standing up for one another."

Samuel says that he and other volunteers have reached out to migrant workers in Little India in the past two years but have always found it a challenge to make a meaningful connection.

"It was always hard to connect on either side. It was as if we were from completely different worlds and in a way, I guess we were. They would become suspicious, so unfamiliar with receiving kindness."

"Now it is as if the doors have been slammed open! I told a group of migrant workers friends, that when this is all over, we are going to grab some dinner. They were so thrilled by that."

Looking ahead

Samuel adds that he is optimistic about the future.

"I'd like to see a new Singapore when all of this is over. I'd love to see foreign workers beginning to become integrated into society. I understand it's hard with cultural differences, but it's the only way to ever understand one another and grow into a higher standard as one people."

When we look at people at a distance, they are a nameless, faceless crowd. But as we get closer, we begin to pick out individuals. They become more "real" to us. Similarly, as we reach out to our fellow residents in Singapore, be they local or foreigner, it becomes easier to empathise with their situation. And that is the most important thing of all.

As Samuel says, "It's the relationship now that is so precious. These guys are no longer people on the other side of the fence. Now I can go up to them and call them 'my brother'."

"We spend our best years in Singapore... I don't want us to feel scared of Singaporeans"

A foreign worker who came to Singapore 10 years ago wants to build bridges between different communities with a library for migrants and cultural events.

by Jamie Wong

"My grandfather is a proud British Indian. My father is a proud Pakistani. And me? I am a Bangladeshi. My family always stayed in the same village, but each generation has a different nationality."

Fazley Elahi Rubel, 30, grew up feeling like a misfit in Bangladesh. Due to constantly changing borders, each of his family members identified with a different nationality. As such, he believes in harmony regardless of race, religion or nationality.

When he was studying in Bangladesh, books in Bengali and English were a way for him to explore the world. He amassed a shelf of books about science and history in his room, and would pick them up to read whenever he craved an adventure.

Fazley in his home town (left) and with family members (right). *Credit: Instagram / Fazley Elahi Rubel.*

His love for reading even led him to start a small library back in his village, but all that had to be left behind when his family hit a financial roadblock.

"The library was already done up, and was just about to officially open, too," he says.

Leaving his parents and five siblings behind, Fazley came to Singapore as a migrant worker around a decade ago, putting a stop to his studies in business management.

Now working as a safety coordinator at a construction company, he has noticed how migrant workers here are afraid to run into Singaporeans. When they get off work, they would avoid the void decks and other public spaces, preferring to stay in their dormitories or within Little India.

He tells The Pride: "We don't hang out where Singaporeans go because we feel scared."

As a result, his fellow colleagues never saw much of Singapore, which didn't sit right with an adventurer like him. Most of the dormitories are also situated very far from Singaporean residential areas, which Fazley notes doesn't allow for much communication and coexistence between locals and migrant workers.

"Every day, they're working and sending money home to their families. That's not what life is. You need to work and enjoy life too."

In a live interview with TEDxNTU, Fazley shared that while the migrant workers had created somewhat of a community in Singapore, they still feel like fish out of water.

He hopes Singaporeans would actively make them feel more welcome, as they had to give up a familiar life just to provide for their families back home.

Fazley at TEDxNTU. *Credit: Instagram / Fazley Elahi Rubel.*

"We spend our best years in Singapore, leaving our families behind to come here and work. We deserve better," he said in the interview.

Uniting the migrant worker community

Life was tough when he first stepped into Singapore.

"It took me seven years to find out where help was," he said, referring to nonprofit organisations that look after migrant workers.

Even then, he noticed that most of the activities being carried out were tailored to workers of individual nationalities, rather than bringing everyone together.

"The Bangladeshis will go for Bangladeshi events, the Thais will go for Thai events… it was all separated."

"Then I thought of my dream to start a library. Why not do it here?"

He saw an opportunity to bring the migrant worker community together through books. Together with two friends, he approached Transient Workers Count Too, who supported them with a space in Little India.

It started as a library meant for Bangladeshi migrant workers, but quickly grew to include other communities. It soon became known as Migrant Library Singapore.

"Some of my friends suggested to keep it as a library for Bangladeshi workers, but I remembered my values. So I chose to open the library to migrant workers from various nations," says Fazley.

The library accepts donations, and is managed by volunteers of different nationalities from the migrant worker community. The library relies heavily on donations; Tamil and Bengali books are especially harder to come by.

He says: "I want it to be a migrant worker's library. So we have books in Bengali, but also English, Thai, Vietnamese, Malay… and we are adding more languages."

Founded in 2017, the library's space was also used to host book sharing events. Mobile libraries visited dormitories to make reading accessible to migrant workers.

Workshops conducted by experts on story writing for poetry and prose were open to all and hosted at a bigger space in Geylang East Public Library. Fazley's boss gives him time to juggle between working and planning for the library's events.

Conducting a workshop. *Credit: Facebook / Migrant Library Singapore.*

Migrant Library dormitory visit. *Image Credit: Facebook / Migrant Library Singapore.*

Up till the pandemic, the library had grown to 700 books, but Covid-19 has hit it hard – it has been closed since the circuit breaker began.

Events were halted and mobile libraries had to be called off as cases surged in the migrant worker dorms.

Fazley himself, who saves up to travel with his close friends, had to put this year's trip on hold. "I even put a picture of my packed bag on my Instagram story," he says.

Despite that, he looks forward to reopening the library once everything is clear. He hopes that the library would grow to be a welcoming place for everyone, migrant workers and locals, regardless of race or nationality.

Books and memories keep him going

Back at his work site at Orchard, Rubel has a space to accommodate some donated English books that couldn't fit into the library. Sometimes after work, he would settle down to read them. He is a fan of books about history, science and action-filled thrillers.

His favourite book is Yuval Noah Harari's *Sapiens: A Brief History of Humankind*, a book that documents the major developments of humans.

"It reminds me that we are all one race: the human race," he says with a smile.

He also has a library of memories stored in his phone, mostly about his travels with a close friend. He recalls trips to Langkawi and Bintan fondly, where the two of them went on mangrove tours and enjoyed each other's company with good-natured humour.

"I want to make travel videos and put them on YouTube someday," he says. "I want to show my friends and other migrant workers that life can be fun."

Apart from the library, Fazley also kickstarted the Migrant Cultural Show Singapore, a platform for migrant workers to showcase their culture. With the pandemic, the show went virtual in June.

Participants at the Migrant Cultural Show. *Credit: Instagram / Fazley Elahi Rubel.*

Fazley hopes to promote intercultural awareness with his projects, and bridge the gap between the local community and migrant workers.

That's why this year's show was titled 'The Bridge', as it was the first to showcase both migrant and Singaporean artists. The show spotlights migrant culture through music, dance and poetry.

It is his dream to bring people together, whatever their circumstances, wherever he goes.

"My name is Fazley Elahi, it means 'to own big things'. I like to think I own a big heart."

Celebrating the
Singapore spirit

What makes me a Singaporean?

Where does race, culture and nationality figure in a person's identity? What about life stories or overseas experiences? Where is home, truly?

by Li Woon Churdboonchart

Growing up (and even today), I was constantly challenged by the people around me about my identity.

"No, no, you are not a Singaporean! You are a Thai! You have a Thai surname and you don't look like a Singaporean. And you don't talk like a Singaporean!" Granted, it was done in good humour and respectfully, out of curiosity and not malice, but it still triggered many questions in me.

I still remember a little game that my primary school friends and I played during our PSLE breaks – Miss Universe! While everyone was fighting for the make-belief crown, choosing the country that they wanted to represent to have the highest chances of winning, I

A "Miss Universe" contestant and I along the classroom corridor where we practised our "catwalk". *Credit: Li Woon Churdboonchart.*

was constantly switching between being Miss Singapore and Miss Thailand. My 12-year-old self decided that I had to be "fair" to both countries since I am half-half – "a mixed blood".

In secondary school, I remember telling a girlfriend that I suspected that I was a "Eurasian" as no definition that I knew in English could properly describe me. Even the Peranakans have their own unique identity in Singapore so why not a Thai-Singapore mix?

An ideological identity crisis

When I started work, I was "properly classified" as *luk chin* (Thai and Chinese mix) rather than *luk khrueng* (Thai and foreign blood mix) by my Thai colleagues. It was so nice to feel at home when I could communicate in Thai with them – it's like our secret language!

Nowadays, many taxi uncles would mistake me as a Chinese or Taiwanese because my Mandarin makes me sound non-Singaporean. Funnily enough, sometimes I get asked if I am from Japan or Korea because my English accent doesn't have any hint of Singlish. In China, my Chinese friends asked me to identify myself as 北方人 (*bei fang ren*, or Northerner) as my Mandarin accent would fit better and I wouldn't be treated as a 海外华侨 (*hai wai hua qiao*, or overseas Chinese) or a tourist.

When I am in Singapore, people think I am Thai or Taiwanese or Chinese or Japanese or Korean, but never a Singaporean. When I am in Thailand, most people accept me as a Thai as I can get by with my very limited Thai. When I am in a non-Asian country, I am just a non-local, no matter how much I try to integrate into their cultural and social norms.

So what am I? And most importantly, where would I call home?

Many life experiences have shaped me – some good, and some not so pleasant. My experiences as an Australian permanent resident for six years and a student in the UK for a year made me realise what I am and what home means.

In Australia, my Thai friends claimed ownership over me, and "fought" with my Asian friends who could appreciate the fact that I am Singaporean. My non-Asian friends just thought I was Chinese because "isn't Singapore part of China?" I still remember pointing out our little island on the world map to convince an African friend that there is such a country called Singapore!

With my MBA classmates when I was studying in Bath, UK in 2003.
Credit: Li Woon Churdboonchart.

The more I began to defend my identity, the clearer it got for me. I realised that I am not even a *luk chin* by the strictest definition as I don't have a single drop of "authentic" Thai blood – my dad is Thai Chinese (Hainanese), and my mama is a Singaporean Chinese (Hainanese)!

So at least, I've got one part of the equation sorted. I am a true blue Hainanese – and that defines my heritage, culture and practices. My paternal grandfather decided to root himself in Thailand, while my maternal grandfather settled in Singapore. Both of them went down south from Hainan island during the 1930s in search of a better life, a better home. So where is home for me – Singapore born and bred, but with a Thai surname and an Australian PR?

Defining moments

The defining moments were slowly and surely building up when I was in Perth from 1994 to 2000.

I still remember my family (my mum, brothers, cousin and I) had to fight racism every single day being a minority race in Australia. It became worse when right-wing populist Pauline Hanson started her nationalist political party in 1997.

All of this we had to silently endure as immigrants. I guess the final straw for me came when I witnessed first hand how the Asian

With a Thai friend in high school in Perth who acknowledged me only as a Thai! *Credit: Li Woon Churdboonchart.*

community – Indian, Chinese and immigrants from other parts of Asia – was used as chess pieces to gain Asian votes in guild and state politics. I realised then that we weren't being acknowledged as equals, but treated rather as second-class citizens.

It really started me thinking – why would I want to contribute to a country where not everyone treats me as a fellow 子民 (*zi min*, or citizen)? Yes, I had a great future in Australia and could easily get any job through the network that I had built within the Chinese community there, but was Australia really the place I wanted to be for the rest of my life?

Coming home

Luckily, when I was at that crossroads, my mama reminded me that it was time to come home. Yes, HOME.

Singapore is my home and I am forever grateful for the great headstart in life. After spending time overseas, I've come to appreciate its world-class education system, its safe and secure environment even on quiet streets late at night, and how it looks out for my interests and well-being with no discrimination from anyone who chooses this country as their own.

Even if I argue with fellow Singaporeans of all different races, religions and cultures till our faces turn blue, we'd always argue based on facts and on equal grounds.

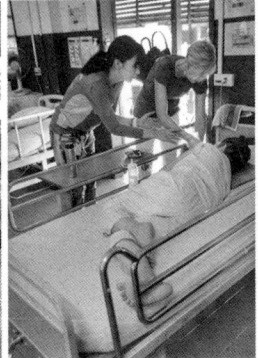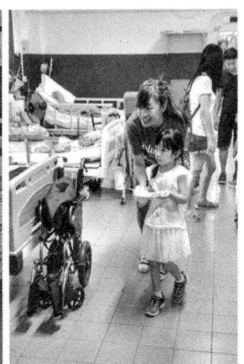

Volunteering in Singapore as part of the Volunteer Switchboard.
Credit: Amalus Barakna.

Unlike some of my experiences overseas, we never crossed the lines as we valued our racial and religious harmony above our differences in opinions. This is what a home should be – we can argue with our closest ones like crazy but we are still a family because blood is thicker than water! Remember that family is the basic unit of a society. We are a big family on a tiny island!

I have realised that being a Singaporean goes beyond how we look and how we speak. It is so much deeper. We are all so diverse but yet we have learnt to appreciate each other (not merely tolerate *ah*), and give each other community support and respect for individuals.

We should focus on our commonalities to make sure that we have cohesion and consensus, and not conflict. We would also 尽地主之谊 (*jin di zhu zhi yi*, or be a gracious host) to the people who make this their home away from home, while they contribute to our nation too. My mama always says, we need to treat everyone kindly as they are after all, someone else's son or daughter.

Yes, Singapore has its imperfections, but hey! no one, and no country is perfect! We have to accept the good and the bad, and make it even better together! We have been blessed with a lot more than most people in other countries, and I am eternally grateful to this little red dot.

So, when I came home from Australia in 2000, I decided to give back to this country and its people as much as I could (that's how I started my volunteering journey with The Volunteer Switchboard).

After all, there's a Chinese saying, 取之社会 用之社会 (*qu zhi she hui, yong zhi she hui* or whatever you have received from society, you should use it for society). I may be a global citizen with many amazing friends all over the world, but Singapore will forever be my home.

In Chinese, 国家 (*guo jia*) means country. The literal translation of each character is 国 = Country, 家 = Home. I've always believed in the Chinese saying that goes 有国才有家 (*you guo cai you jia*), which means only when you have a country, then will you have a home. Some of my friends have argued that it should be the other way round – 有家才有国, that is, only when you focus on family, then will you have a country.

And I challenge them, the sequence wouldn't matter if you make Singapore your home. And if that doesn't convince them, I remind them of the selfless spirit of our frontliners when they put their lives on the line to fight Covid-19 to protect our nation and its people. These courageous silent heroes really showed us what it means to love our Singapore and put the nation above community, and society above self.

Singapore has taken care of me since I was born, and now it's my turn to protect my home and its people.

What makes you Singaporean? What makes Singapore your home (or home away from home)?

For Singaporeans living overseas, is Singapore really home, truly?

Overseas Singaporeans share what makes Singapore home this National Day.

by Serene Leong

A few days ago, like many families, I hung the Singapore flag outside my window in celebration of Singapore's upcoming 55th National Day. Having lived in Singapore all my life, I am proud to call Singapore my home.

More than 217,000 Singaporeans living overseas, however, will be missing out on seeing our city bathed in a sea of red and white this year. While this might be stating the obvious, unlike previous years, some may not have had a choice to return, as the threat of Covid-19 continues to restrict travel.

I spoke with three overseas Singaporeans to find out their thoughts on what makes Singapore home.

Leanne Lim, 29, Melbourne, Australia: "When you come back... it feels like you belong."

Leanne is no stranger to the work that goes behind building our nation. Having moved to Melbourne almost three years ago because of an overseas posting, her work at the Singapore Global Network involves building a community among overseas Singaporeans and friends of Singapore.

"No matter how many years you've been overseas, or how far away you are, there's always something that links you back to Singapore," Leanne tells The Pride.

Even though she is in Melbourne with her husband, Emmanuel, 32, it is the rest of her family, friends and community that keep

Leanne at the Hanging Rock in Victoria. *Credit: Leanne Lim.*

the fires for home burning, as she says most of her memories and identity have been shaped by the character-forming years she spent growing up in Singapore.

Leanne adds: "It's the familiarity and comfort. Things in Singapore are always changing. There are always new buildings, malls and eateries. But by and large, it's still very familiar. It's hard to describe, but it's just the feeling when you are back… when you talk to the food stall aunty or the bus driver. It feels like you belong."

But there is also much that she misses from not being here. She misses the food, but it's not just about the dishes, she says. It is sharing a meal with her family and friends back home.

She also misses normal everyday activities like walking to her neighbourhood coffee shop. "It's not like the nearest coffee shop will have the best food but I think it's just the nostalgia of doing things I used to do," she says.

Leanne has also come to appreciate how easy it is to *makan* back home, with some coffee shops open 24 hours and curry puffs or *kueh* just a stroll away at the neighbourhood shopping mall basement. In Melbourne, cafés usually close by 3pm.

Despite this, she says that the city is very multicultural and there are a wide range of cuisines. "With a lot of migration, the food also gets better. We eat more dumplings here than in Singapore!"

Leanne was last back in Singapore for a short visit during Chinese New Year in January 2020, and since she returned to Australia, this is the longest she has been away from home – she usually comes back with her husband once a year and another once or twice alone for work.

Leanne says: "What's worse is not so much how long it's been since I visited, but looking ahead to how long more it will be until I see Singapore again… that feels a bit sad."

With stricter travel restrictions and border closures as Melbourne enters a second lockdown, she has no idea when they will be able to return.

But that will not stop her from tuning in to the National Day activities in Singapore.

"Some of my friends in Singapore are having a small gathering so I'll probably Zoom in so that I can sing along!"

Deepa Kumaran, 32, Jubail, Saudi Arabia: "In Singapore, you have security, you're not worried."

Deepa has been working offshore as a project engineer for an oil company in Jubail, Saudi Arabia for almost two years. Every morning, he drives 20 minutes from his residence and takes a boat to a vessel where he works.

When he first arrived in the country, Deepa had to quickly adapt to the cultural differences. Men have to wear trousers when they go out, and women have to be completely covered up in public. Women and men eat separately in eateries, unless they are a family. The Saudis pray five times a day, and everything – even the supermarkets and restaurants – closes for half an hour each time.

Deepa tells The Pride: "You need to know all these rules, because if you break them, the police can catch you. They're quite strict. If you get caught with alcohol, which is banned, you will go to jail."

Deepa (far left) with his colleagues at their work site in Jubail. *Credit: Deepa Kumaran.*

"When you work overseas, it's different because you are a foreigner. Especially with security. Some of the police don't speak English so if anything happens, it's very hard to communicate."

He recalls that once, his colleagues were taken to the police station because they did not have their passport with them when they went out and could not explain their situation because they could not speak Arabic.

When Covid-19 hit, Deepa says that the country tightened its restrictions – flights were reduced and only locals were allowed to travel in and out of the country. There were also curfews where residents could only go out from 6am to 3pm.

Naturally, Deepa had concerns about safety. What if there was an emergency at home and he could not fly back? With only about 150 Singaporeans in Jubail, there was only one rescue flight in April, but Deepa says that at the time he was busy with work, so he chose to stay.

He says: "When Covid first started, I didn't know how equipped their hospitals were. What if I really got Covid? In Singapore, you know you are safe because our hospitals are first class. That's when I realised medical security is important."

Fortunately, Deepa says that the Saudi government has been efficient in dealing with the crisis. Sanitisation is done regularly, and the Saudi King has offered to finance treatment for anyone infected with the coronavirus in the country. The Singapore embassy staff also call to check in on him and update him often.

His project is ending soon but Deepa wonders when he can return home. It is not so straightforward, he says.

"If flights open up, hopefully I can fly back. It's not easy to get on to the rescue flights. There will be only four or five seats. So it's fastest fingers first."

As for what he misses most about Singapore: "Food," he says, without missing a beat. "Middle Eastern food gets boring after a month, especially when you are Singaporean and you have so much variety at home," Deepa says. "For example, it's very hard to find Japanese food, and when you do, it doesn't even taste Japanese!"

Deepa also can't wait to meet up with his friends. "There is no social life here. This year, they just opened their first cinema. But it closed because of Covid, so I didn't get a chance to go."

Half-jokingly, he says: "I want to come home. Job finishing already. I'm afraid my boss will cut my salary."

Greg Low, 34, Hong Kong: "Home is not a particular country or place, it is where my family is."

Being born in Singapore and having lived in four other countries – the US, Canada, Greece and Hong Kong, not to mention two years of living on a ship – makes Greg's story a unique one.

He is now living and working in Hong Kong with his wife, Suanne, 34, and their two daughters, Kharis, three, and Hara, one. The family moved from Greece to Suanne's home country last year because Hara had a heart defect and Hong Kong offers cheaper and better medical care and support.

Having spent more time overseas than in Singapore, it is not a surprise that Greg says he does not consider Singapore – or any particular country – home.

He tells The Pride: "After living in so many countries, anywhere can be home, it just depends where your family is. We have a family culture that's not defined by where we are from but what we have experienced [multiculturally] and what we want our kids to be."

Greg says that his varied experiences have taught him that there are good values in different cultures. As parents, he and his wife want to take these positive values from different cultures, for example, racial and religious harmony in Singapore, and apply them wherever they raise their children.

Greg, his wife Suanne, and their two daughters Kharis and Hara. *Credit: Greg Low.*

He says that despite the similarities between Hong Kong and Singapore, he took a while to adjust to life there.

"Hong Kong is a bit more about efficiency so at first I was a bit slow. The pace of life is slower in Singapore and Singaporeans tend to value relationships with people over the work that needs to get done."

It is also a different kind of neighbourhood that he lives in. Greg explains that unlike Singapore, where there are different races mingling in each HDB estate, in Hong Kong, there are mostly just Chinese and foreigners.

"You talk more to your neighbours in Singapore because you spend more time at home. In Hong Kong the apartments are so small that you just go home to sleep."

He speaks both English and Cantonese. And he laughs when I ask if his wife has learnt anything Singaporean from him.

"I think she has more of a Singaporean accent than me," he says. "It's because of Singlish. Her best friend is Malaysian."

Singapore, to Greg and his family, is more of a place where they visit his parents.

Do his kids know they are Singaporean?

"Not really," Greg says. "My first daughter was born in Greece, raised in Hong Kong, but she is a Singaporean. As a third culture kid it's not so easy. We will let them decide on their own identity when they are older."

Even though Singapore is less of a home to him, Greg says that he may still tune in with his family to watch the parade on National Day. Or take a walk down memory lane by listening to acapella versions of NDP songs from over the years – from 1962's "Singapura" to 2001's "Where I Belong" – to get into the patriotic mood.

No matter where we are on Aug 9, there is one thing aside from the colour of our passports that connects us as One People, One Nation and One Singapore. We are part of our little red dot no matter where we are on our huge blue planet. And that sense of home is what truly makes us Singaporean.

193 countries in 17 years: Lessons this Singaporean learnt from visiting every country in the world

She travels the world to find a universal truth – that love, kindness and compassion exist in all cultures regardless of race, language or economic status.

by Serene Leong

She is the first Asian woman to visit every sovereign country and the first Singaporean to have visited all United Nations member states.

In 2017, at the age of 37, Yui Pow-Redford made history by travelling to 193 countries in 17 years, mostly solo.

Her journey has taken her to big cities and small towns, affluent economies and underdeveloped nations, and literally to the ends of the earth – the North and South Poles.

Admiring the vastness of the Sahara – Chinguetti, Mauritania in northwestern Africa. *Credit: Yui Pow-Redford.*

Meeting the Huli tribe, Tari Highlands, Papua New Guinea.
Credit: Yui Pow-Redford.

While travelling has enabled her to experience different cultures, make sense of the world, and given her life skills not taught in the classroom, it has also gifted her something precious – an appreciation of our human connection.

Yui tells The Pride: "Wherever you go, people are intrigued by others who are different. At the same time they're happy to discover someone is interested in their culture and they like it when you find something in common with them."

"I found that values like love, kindness, compassion and empathy exist in all cultures of the world and they are universal."

A desire for knowledge

The daughter of a pilot father and a scuba-diving mother, Yui developed a passion for travel from an early age.

Yui did most of her travels while based in London, where she lives with her 44-year-old husband. Born and bred in Singapore, she did her degree in the US, worked in Tokyo for a couple of years, completed her masters in London and has lived there since.

The language consultant, who has knowledge of about 25 languages, says that achieving her feat was a juggling act because she worked throughout the 17 years, which meant she could not be continuously on the road.

Her trips would usually last between three to ten weeks at a time and would span multiple countries. Running her own business meant that she was able to work from any location in the world and plan her work around her travels.

Yui's first big solo trip covered the Trans-Siberian Railway, the Chinese Silk Road, and the Karakoram Highway through Pakistan before crossing into India.

> "I found that values like love, kindness, compassion and empathy exist in all cultures of the world and they are universal."

Her journey started out of a curiosity to see the world, Yui says.

"It wasn't for a record or achievement. It was an attempt to get to know the different parts of the world and the cultures better… and it tied in with my language work. It was a good chance to practise it and to see how people on the ground communicate."

"If you asked me at age 25 or 30 if I planned to [visit every country in the world], I would probably say no. I didn't even consider it until I reached about 120 countries, then I thought why not try to do it all?" Yui says.

The cultural divide

Over the years, Yui says that she has gotten an appreciation of the similarities, differences and patterns between cultures. One of the heartening things she has noticed is that many of the similarities in cultures are related to the human condition.

"Besides needs like clothing, food and shelter, most people want to be loved and they have the capacity to love," she says.

"Across cultures, people value family and education, they want to better themselves. No matter where they are in life, they want to accomplish something."

Kindness takes many forms

Over the years, Yui has experienced countless acts of kindness from locals and strangers.

"It can be as simple as someone giving you something on the house, or going out of their way to help you, or just a friendly smile or greeting. I'm always grateful for those types of actions, but it means a lot more when people don't expect anything in return."

Once, she was in Sierra Leone, in West Africa, one of the poorest countries in the world, when she got caught in a precarious situation. "I was walking on the roadside at night when I got targeted by a group of youths who tried to attack me and steal my valuables. I was basically surrounded – there were a few youths behind and in front of me, they were across the road and alongside me trying to make conversation and jostle me. There was no way I could have escaped."

"But in the nick of time, a car pulled up. A passing couple had noticed what was happening and they shouted at the youths and put a stop to it."

Yui says the couple then told her to get into their car and took her safely to her next destination.

They wouldn't allow Yui to pay them or buy them a meal, so all she could do was send them a text to thank them for saving her life.

Yui says: "I couldn't believe that they would stop for a stranger… they didn't have to do it. It was one of the incidents that restored my faith in humanity."

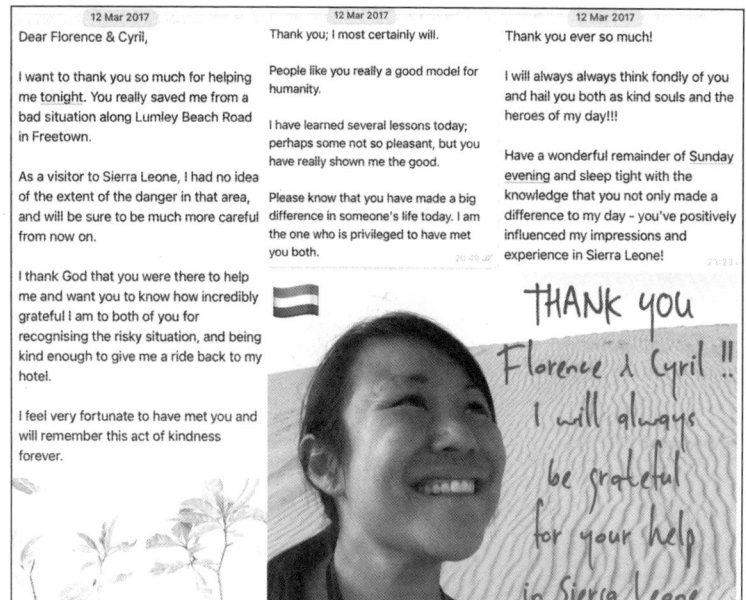

A message of thanks. *Credit: Yui Pow-Redford.*

Yui, her guide and his family in Tripoli, Libya. *Credit: Yui Pow-Redford.*

Friendships around the world

It isn't only the big gestures that Yui remembers. Other instances of kindness that she has received include people sharing what little food they had and even inviting her into their homes!

She recalls one such family in Libya – the father-of-four was her guide in the country – who opened up their simple home to her.

Thanks to the Internet, she is still in touch with the family today – and many others.

"It's a nice relationship even if it's just greetings from time to time."

Yui adds that since the pandemic started and international travel came to a halt, many friends from all over the world have reached out to her.

Yui is still in contact with the friends from Sweden, UK and Venezuela that she made on her Arctic trip in Svalbard. *Credit: Yui Pow-Redford.*

"I've had people from the Carribean Islands send a message to ask 'How is it over there? Hope you are doing fine.'"

Yui says that she organises her contact list in order of country because of all the friends she has made through her travels! However, she says that not all connections progress into long-term friendships. Sometimes, it's more of a temporary bond.

Still, she says: "It's a beautiful thing and that's something that travel gives you. The chance to connect with others."

Solo travel has its rewards

As a solo female traveller (for most of her journeys), one of Yui's biggest challenges is safety.

Getting scammed and robbed are a reality that every traveller in the rough has had to deal with; and there were several incidents where Yui had her phone and valuables stolen, despite taking the necessary precautions.

Yui admits: "It does put a dampener on your trip and the views you have of that country. But I've got over them by thinking that it doesn't necessarily mean that the person is evil or mean. Many of these scams stem from the hustling they need to do to survive and the way they live their lives. I'd like to believe that this is because they don't live in the same circumstances as a person from a more affluent country."

Friends from Germany, Uruguay and Guyana on a boat off an island in Belize.
Credit: Yui Pow-Redford.

"You have to go with an open mind. If you think that the world is full of evil people, then you will miss out on a lot of the rewarding experiences."

Another challenge Yui faced on the road is loneliness.

While her husband accompanied her to places such as South America and Scandinavia, Yui said that she sometimes wished she had someone to share the experience on the road.

She says: "It's quite lonely to travel by yourself because we all crave human connection. It's nice to be able to share the experiences like if you see a beautiful sunset or are enjoying a nice meal."

However, Yui says that she overcame her loneliness by reframing her mindset to see solitude as an opportunity to reflect on her life and circumstances and to become more independent.

A lifelong education

For Yui, travel has given her the best all-rounded education.

"It's almost like taking an extended course on the ways of the world!" she says, adding that she has learnt about history, geography, sociology, among other things. Being able to experience a country firsthand helps what she reads on the news, like food, religion, sport and politics, take on a greater significance and helps her relate to those she meets.

In a classroom during a school visit in Banjul, Gambia. *Credit: Yui Pow-Redford.*

Distributing gifts and supplies in Morondava, Madagascar. *Credit: Yui Pow-Redford.*

Travel has also given her a greater awareness of and empathy towards the world.

"I realised that I can make a difference in someone's life somewhere. And that a very little can go a long way… It doesn't really cost a lot of money to be kind," Yui says.

Giving back to the global community

It is with this belief that Yui started Goodyus, a non-profit entity that supports charities worldwide through fundraising, volunteering, skills-sharing and donation of materials.

She recalls: "On my first trip to Tanzania, Africa, in 2013 where I climbed Mount Kilimanjaro, they suggested for us to bring along some items to give to the porters, the climbing team and the cooks. I packed some spare hats, gloves and T-shirts."

"When I presented these gifts to the locals after the climb, they were so grateful and happy. It made me think, 'how many of us have items that are collecting dust in our wardrobes when they could be used by someone else around the world?'"

"Goodyus grew from the belief that every resource – not just material possessions but also time, money and skills – might be able to help somebody in need."

This year, due to Covid-19, support for Goodyus has mostly been in the form of donations to Covid-relief causes.

Making a connection, Phobjikha Valley, Bhutan. *Credit: Yui Pow-Redford.*

Yui says Goodyus has also supported schools by donating digital materials and sharing curriculum and worksheets she designed to help students from emerging countries with their language skills.

Home is where the heart is

Now that Yui has completed her mission, what's next?

"Besides working on Goodyus, I'm spending a lot of time learning languages because I hope to travel the world through them," she says, adding that she also devotes more time to her two other passions – music and writing.

And for someone who has been to all the countries in the world, where would she choose to live?

Yui says that travelling and living in all these places has completely altered her concept of home.

"A lot of people think home is a place, but for me I would say home is more of a state of mind. It's a place where I feel comfortable and happy, a place where I can return to anytime and it's familiar."

"Where would I live? I am quite happy where I am now. Or I would say Singapore. I love the food. You can take me out of Asia but you can't really take Asia out of me! Singapore is somewhere I would always be very happy."

Let's celebrate racial harmony during the Festival of Lights

Teaching cultural awareness in schools is good, but we can take it one step further by embracing racial harmony the kampung way - through food and friends.

by Karun S'Baram

As one of the major cultural festivals in Singapore, Deepavali (also known as Diwali or the Festival of Lights) is a celebration that marks the triumph of good over evil.

It's when thousands of Hindu families, in our country and across the world, transform their homes into beacons of light and share feasts with families and friends.

I'll always remember the breakfasts my mum would make when I was a young boy – *thosai* with chicken curry that we'll wolf down before putting on our new clothes. I also remember Deepavali for the shopping! It is the norm to wear new clothes on the day of celebration as it marks respect and excitement for the festival.

I guess that's why it's a common misconception in Singapore for my non-Indian friends to wish us a "Happy New Year" on that day. Deepavali isn't the Hindu new year. In fact, Puthandu, as it is called, falls on Apr 14 every year, which coincides with the famous Thai water festival Songkran.

It's hard not to notice a Hindu home during Deepavali, especially back in my kampung days. Each doorway would boast a *rangoli* – a beautiful, vividly-coloured artwork created out of flour, rice or flower petals – which blesses the household for the year ahead.

In primary school, our children are taught and tested on the importance and significance of many of our cultural festivities. I daresay that they would celebrate them with as much enthusiasm as any child would have for any day that they didn't have to go to school!

But is there more to racial harmony than just finding out how friends from different cultures celebrate their special days? For example, do our kids know that Indians in Singapore consist of a range of different groups including Tamils and Malayalees, or that being an Indian in Singapore doesn't automatically make you a Hindu?

For that matter, do our non-Chinese Singaporean friends know the significance and importance of Qingming? Or do non-Malays immediately know the difference between Hari Raya Puasa and Hari Raya Haji without having to google it?

Back in the 80s, without the distractions of social media (and Netflix!), I spent the majority of my growing-up years in the company of my kampung kakis. And it was with this band of multi-racial brothers that I learnt, firsthand, with no textbook or search engine in sight, how to grow up in a multicultural society.

James

I got to know James from a schoolmate. James was from a different secondary school but we connected as he lived in my neighbourhood.

James had his own room and a computer (back in the 80s, having an XT, a 286 or, gasp, a 386! made you a king among mortals) and that was one of the reasons we always ended up at his place to play computer games (helloooo Lode Runner!).

Often, I would help James with his homework and his parents always rewarded me by inviting me to stay for dinner. With them, I

Growing up with my band of ethnic brothers (from left, Ben, James, Karun, Justin and Jun Jie). *Credit: Karun S'Baram.*

had my first steamboat, my first *bak kut teh* and my first (and last) century egg – I did not enjoy that one!

His family, who were Taoists, had ancestral tablets inscribed with their forefathers' names on an altar that you cannot miss the moment you step into his home. I learnt that filial piety and ancestral worship were very important to his family.

I also learnt about Qingming, a day to remember the dead. Along with many Taoists in Singapore, every April 4 or 5, James and his family would visit the tombs of their ancestors and clean the gravesite as a mark of respect.

Taoists also believe that on the 15th day of the 7th lunar month, spirits leave the netherworld to roam the world. Because of this belief, many folks will pray to the wandering spirits and lost souls on this day and over time it has become the Chinese tradition and festival (*getai* and all) that we all know today – The Hungry Ghost Festival.

I remember how during that month, James hardly went out at night!

I enjoyed my time with James and his family and still fondly remember the experiences I had with them and the education they left with me.

Imran

I got to know Imran in my secondary school days. He was from an older cohort and we became good friends as we both played rugby and football together.

Imran stayed across the school and always invited a few of us over. One thing I loved about going to Imran's place was the food! I love spicy food and his grandmother cooked the best – not only tasting but also looking – dishes!

It was at Imran's that I learnt about *sambal* – not just *sambal* but its variations.

Let's start with *sambal tumis*, this *sambal* is a staple for many of us because it's the perfect condiment for *nasi lemak*. But Imran's grandmother will say "if it looks bright red, then it is not *sambal tumis*. It's probably *sambal belachan*".

Belachan is the perfect accompaniment for rice dishes. Then there is also *sambal hijau*, and *sambal kicap* which many of us will remember growing up eating with sour mangoes and guava.

I also learnt the importance of and the differences between Hari Raya Puasa and Hari Raya Haji. On Hari Raya Puasa, Muslims visit relatives and friends for a day of feasting. On Hari Raya Haji, a *korban* (sacrifice) is performed.

Hari Raya Puasa is celebrated at the end of the Ramadan fasting month, Hari Raya Haji is celebrated 70 days later at the end of the *hajj* (pilgrimage). Every able-bodied and financially able Muslim is obliged to make the pilgrimage to Mecca at least once in their life.

At Imran's, Hari Raya Puasa was always a feast to remember.

Rodney

During my primary school days (oh those primary school days!), I made my first best friend, Rodney Oliveiro. Rodney was taller and bigger than most boys in my cohort and he was a big brother to all of us. We were in the same class from Primary 3 to 6 and became best buds.

I remember having this very tangy meat curry, which I later found out was called devil's curry, at Rodney's place during a Christmas gathering. Devil's curry is a spicy curry, usually made with chicken and flavoured with vinegar.

While often cooked throughout the year, it is traditionally served at festive occasions celebrated by Eurasian communities, often complete with alcohol and someone's brother or uncle strumming a guitar. Without Rodney, I would have missed out savouring this

Rodney and me in a photo taken during our school trip to the Botanical Gardens.
Credit: Karun S'Baram.

homemade delicacy and experiencing such warm hospitality at that young age.

Growing up, I had several Eurasian friends who were mostly Catholics.

It was from them that I learnt about the significance of Lent. It is a period of 40 days immediately before Easter, which Christians celebrate as the resurrection of Jesus after his death on the cross.

Lent marks a time of sombre reflection for Catholics to renew their commitment to Christ. During this time, Catholics practise abstinence, including avoiding eating meat on certain days.

It's a big difference from another Christian holiday, Christmas, which doesn't really need an introduction since it has always been widely celebrated in most countries around the world. After all, coming at the end of the year, with school holidays and bonuses, what's not to celebrate?

The Festival of Lights

In northern India, Hindus celebrate the story of King Rama's return to Ayodhya after he defeated Ravana by lighting rows of clay lamps. In southern India, Deepavali is the day that Lord Krishna defeated the demon Narakasura. In western India, the festival marks the day that Lord Vishnu, the Preserver, sent the demon King Bali to rule the netherworld.

Hindus interpret the Deepavali story based on where they live. But there's one common theme that goes through it all. No matter where people celebrate Deepavali, it is about the triumph and the victory of good over evil.

This Deepavali, let's make an effort to understand, accept and embrace our cultures. In Singapore, we have made great strides in building a multicultural society where our children can play together, regardless of race or religion.

For that to continue, it's important to have racial understanding and it should continue outside the classroom. Like me, I hope everyone can find their Jameses, Imrans and Rodneys. I am so glad that I had them growing up.

Racism coloured my childhood and I still fight against stereotypes today

Vietnam-born but raised in Hungary, she experienced racism growing up, and talks about what gives her hope in Singapore – diversity and inclusion.

by Trang Chu Minh

Growing up, racism was a regular part of my life. But while it coloured my childhood, thanks to family and friends, it did not define me. And even though I have become more resilient and compassionate because of it, I have also always battled a sense of "survivor's guilt".

It's no surprise that Singapore, with its multi-ethnic, multi-national societal fabric, immediately felt like a place where I could finally belong.

I have no doubt created my own echo chamber – and safety bubble – of family, friends and colleagues who appreciate and respect diversity and inclusion as much as I do, and my thoughts here by no means negate the issues of systemic racism and racial stereotyping Singapore has long grappled with.

But amidst a tornado of negative news, rather than focusing on problems alone, I wanted to remind everyone of the positive initiatives that you can support or get involved in – the good deeds between locals and foreigners, or people of different ethnicities – and the organisations that empower the vulnerable or the less fortunate.

Experiencing racism first hand

Whilst I have experienced my fair share of racist slurs as the only Asian kid growing up in an ethnically homogenous small town in Hungary, I have always considered myself a person of privilege, and have for the longest time carried an unconscious guilt over what I perceived as undeserved advantage.

I have been hesitant to share my thoughts because amid the current climate defined by an overwhelming sense of division, disillusion and information overload, I wanted to be able to contribute in a constructive manner.

Truth be told, I was also afraid of remembering my past.

As you can tell from my name, I am not Chinese or Japanese, but have learnt Mandarin or Japanese greetings as a child because those were the phrases my bullies shouted at me, no doubt from the many Asian martial arts movies they had watched.

I used to dread the short walk home from primary school, because it meant walking past a worksite with construction workers or a playground with a group of local teens. Always, words and racist names would be thrown at me, and once, even a dead pigeon – which explains my horrendous bird phobia that my friends and family still tease me for!

I had to ignore whispers from fellow students shocked to hear that "a child of immigrant parents who used to work in the Asian market" can win academic competitions or get into university abroad. They didn't bother to find out that my parents – as many Vietnamese immigrants in the 1980s and 90s in Eastern and Central Europe – were former academic scholarship students who grew their now thriving business from humble beginnings as market stallholders.

I lived through many awkward moments at school when teachers had gone to great lengths to publicly express their surprise – in front of entire classes of students – over the fact that I performed well "although I was not Hungarian or ethnically white".

> These stories are of my childhood in Hungary, but they could very well have described incidents of casual racism that many in Singapore may have had to deal with too.

Even after years of studies and training, I have had work calls where male colleagues would make off-handed comments that I was chosen for a project because as a woman of Asian ethnic heritage, I

Graduating with my second Masters with the DBS Top Student Award and as a Dean's List student. *Credit: Trang Chu Minh.*

would tip the scales in terms of diversity and inclusion, or because I was "easy on the eyes". They made zero mention of my relevant professional skills or industry knowledge. The blatant – albeit likely unintended – sexism and tokenism emanating from these words blindsided me.

Questioning my identity – the Imposter Syndrome

Don't get me wrong, I don't mean to focus on the negativity or contribute to the cancel culture that seems so prevalent these days. Often, these comments were made not out of spite, but were nonetheless delivered in a careless manner that made me feel uncomfortable, and have solidified a deep sense of Imposter Syndrome that I have struggled with ever since.

What were intended as light-hearted jokes shook me to the core, and made me question my identity.

Victims of racism and discrimination in Singapore no doubt go through similar emotions of self-doubt, so the reason I am sharing this personal story is to implore anyone who is reading this – if you have even a sliver of doubt over the racist (or sexist) undertones of your joke, just don't say it.

That said, I have grown up in a loving and accepting environment, with friends of all races, nationalities or orientation, and family thriving in all corners of the planet. I have never been discriminated against when it came to the defining moments of my life – throughout my education, at the workplace, or in my personal relationships – nor have I ever felt like I suffered an unfair disadvantage because of the colour of my skin or my gender.

During the countless times we were called out in Hungary for "stealing people's jobs", or were told to "get out of their country", my family always encouraged me to take the high ground, and to let these snide remarks slide. In their view, arguing would not have changed people's perceptions.

Championing diversity and inclusion

Instead, I focused on advocacy for greater diversity and inclusion, whether that related to gender equality, LGBT rights or equal opportunities for those of underprivileged or vulnerable backgrounds.

I am aware that Singapore is far from immune to racial injustice or ethnic nationalism, but the country's staunch commitment to creating a peaceful, multi-ethnic society, along with its vibrant culinary scene (of course!), are some of the reasons why, following stints in Melbourne and London, I have decided to make the city-state my home.

Since living in Singapore and with my journalist hat on, I have continued my hunt for initiatives that empower and support those

My daily coffee run to visit Lucy, a previously homeless person who was trained and employed as a professional barista by London-based social enterprise Change Please. Lucy has since built her first home, learnt English and has a Change Please coffee blend named after her. *Credit: Trang Chu Minh.*

Celebrating the many diversity and inclusion champions in my life on International Women's Day. *Credit: Trang Chu Minh.*

that most need it, and the search has been immensely gratifying.

For anyone who expressed fear over new migrant worker dorms being placed near housing estates, have you read about the foreign worker who risked injury to save a toddler dangling from a second-storey flat, or the Bangladeshi cleaners who helped residents escape a burning HDB flat?

For those in despair over the foreign-local dichotomy in Singapore, have you checked out the welcome notes penned by Singaporeans to show their gratitude and appreciation to foreign workers? Welcome in my backyard (WIMBY) aims to counter NIMBYism ('Not in my backyard'), and bridge the gap between locals and foreigners, through initiatives such as virtual dialogue sessions targeted at debunking myths and misconceptions of foreign workers.

If you recognise the precarious circumstances they live in and work under, would you be keen to volunteer with migrant workers? From teaching financial skills to domestic helpers at Aidha, to providing free medical consultation and counselling to migrant workers through HealthServe, or even simple tasks like packing food with Transient Workers Count Too, the opportunities are endless.

Engaging the Bettr Barista team at a corporate event. *Credit: Trang Chu Minh.*

Moving beyond race to empower the vulnerable

Diversity and inclusion should also go above and beyond issues of race or nationality, and what you choose to spend your bucks on can make a whole lot of difference.

I know that many of us are itching to enjoy our favourite food fixes as businesses reopen during Phase 2, but would you consider going to restaurants, cafés or bakeries that employ or train people with special needs or from challenging backgrounds?

Have you visited Dignity Kitchen, a food court in Serangoon that trains and employs those with disabilities or from disadvantaged circumstances on the ins-and-outs of running a hawker stall?

Would you consider engaging Hush TeaBar for a team-building activity? The social enterprise trains and employs people with hearing impairments or mental health issues to perform tea rituals using sign language.

Have you ordered flowers from BloomBack, which provides skills training and employment to marginalised groups, and upcycles blooms from events as donations to homes and hospices?

Would you get a cuppa from Bettr Barista, which trains at-risk youth and women as baristas, or Foreword Coffee, which provides inclusive employment opportunities to people with disabilities?

Have you gotten your mani-pedi done at Nail Social, a socially conscious salon which works with marginalized women with a higher barrier to employment?

There are many other social enterprises and conscious businesses that are worth supporting. All it takes is for you to look out for them.

Racism and inequality are real struggles that ought to be discussed more transparently and tackled more actively, but the organisations that aim to make Singapore a more diverse and inclusive society should equally be applauded.

If there is one thing to take away from this article, I hope it's for people to think carefully about how they too can (and should) tackle racial injustice, and inequality in general.

Whether it's to call out inappropriate jokes in your circles; push for (a more robust) diversity and inclusion policy at your workplace that's properly enforced and audited; advocate for more inclusive government policies; or volunteer with organisations that support vulnerable communities, we each have a role to play.

Can a UNESCO listing keep Singapore's hawker culture alive?

Singapore hawker culture is now officially on the UNESCO Intangible Cultural Heritage list – a first for Singapore! But are hawker centres in danger of dying out?

by Serene Leong

"What shall we eat for dinner tonight?"

It is the perennial question my husband and I ask each other nowadays, more so since we've been working from home. Often, the answer is "*dapao* downstairs" or "order delivery".

Since Covid, we have gotten lazier. We rarely eat out, and when we do – usually on weekends like many millennials – we enjoy exploring trendy cafés in our neighbourhood.

So when I suggested having dinner at Bukit Timah food centre one recent Saturday, he was surprised. But the thought of savouring local delights such as hokkien mee, fried carrot cake, barbecued chicken wings and satay – not forgetting iced chendol! – only made our mouths water.

Tucking into my favourite hawker dishes. *Credit: Serene Leong.*

The queues are back at hawker centres. *Credit: Serene Leong.*

Singapore's community dining rooms

On Dec 16, 2020, it was announced that Singapore's hawker culture is now on the UNESCO Representative List of the Intangible Cultural Heritage of Humanity – a first for Singapore – joining more than 460 other cultural practices that define communities in our globalised world, including yoga in India and Belgian beer.

Hawker culture is a defining aspect of our national identity. In his National Day Rally 2018, Prime Minister Lee Hsien Loong termed our hawker centres "community dining rooms" that bring together people of all ages, ethnicities and cultural backgrounds.

But then again, you don't need our PM to tell us what we already know. Visit any hawker centre and you will see a melting – no, *makan* – pot of cultures, both literally and figuratively.

Its affordability also makes it a great equaliser of income. It is not uncommon to see white-collar executives rubbing shoulders with retirees, or blue-collar artisans jostling with families with young children.

In a 2018 National Heritage Board poll of 3,000 people, "food heritage" was voted the most important aspect of Singapore's intangible cultural heritage.

Similarly, a 2016 survey by the National Environment Agency revealed that nine in every 10 Singaporeans feel that hawker centres are an important part of Singapore's identity, while 75% said they visit a hawker centre as least once a week.

A comforting Singapore scene. *Credit: Serene Leong.*

There is possibly nothing closer that so quintessentially defines our Singapore identity.

Even a scene in Hollywood rom-com *Crazy Rich Asians* featured lead characters Rachel and her boyfriend Nick meeting up with some friends over satay and sambal stingray at Newton Food Centre after they land in Singapore!

Just think about the last time you were overseas (I know, it's been a while). What was the first thing you craved when you stepped foot back on our sunny island? Chances are, you were thinking of your favourite hawker dish (it's hokkien mee for me).

We love hawker food, but do we treasure it?

With cosy cafés, high-end restaurants and bars slowly colonising our neighbourhoods, it's easy to see why younger Singaporeans don't think about meeting up at hawker centres.

We proudly proclaim our love and pride for local makan, but rather fork out more than $20 for an eggs benedict or chilli crab linguine.

Today, the median age of hawkers is 60. Many are finding it hard to pass on the trade as younger adults are less willing to become hawkers, partly due to longer working hours, perceived lower social status, and hard work involved.

Some young chefs have left corporate jobs and taken up the mantle as hawkerpreneurs; however, they are the exception rather than the norm.

I noticed that most of the hawkers at Bukit Timah food centre are older Singaporeans, with many stalls run by migrant workers.

As my husband and I squeezed through the throng of people that Saturday, something felt different. It was almost impossible to keep a safe distance from people while looking for a table and queueing for food.

Orange nettings marked almost half the seats. Every few minutes, an automated broadcast message reminding diners to return their trays and wear their masks when not eating and drinking was repeated in three languages.

Hawkers have not been spared from the effects of Covid-19. They were one of the hardest hit groups, especially during the circuit breaker when dining in was not allowed and stalls had to rely on takeaways and deliveries to survive.

Thankfully, since Phase 2, some of the bustle has returned to hawker centres as business continues to improve, albeit at a slower pace. And with Phase 3 on the horizon, things are looking on the up.

Aside from Covid challenges, the inherent problems of being a hawker haven't changed over the years.

They still have to balance high rental costs while keeping prices affordable, although in recent years, the government has introduced several schemes to help.

Then, there is the problem of patrons not returning their trays. It may not directly impact hawkers' livelihoods, but it certainly affects the ambience.

How many times have you found a table at a hawker centre or food court, only to be greeted with the sight of chicken bones and used tissues on dirty plates?

CNA reported last month that despite the Return-Your-Tray initiative that was rolled out in 2013 and updated again this year, it is common to see a majority of diners leaving their trays behind after meals.

Which begs the question, are we too reliant on our cleaners?

Recently, Minister for Sustainability and the Environment Grace Fu cited a Singapore Management University (SMU) survey where one in three respondents felt it was the cleaner's job to return trays.

The common argument for this is that cleaners may lose their jobs if we return our trays for them. But that's a logical fallacy.

Celebrating the Singapore spirit

Let's use the tray return stations and not leave our mess behind for our hardworking cleaners. *Credit: Serene Leong.*

Returning our trays does not deprive cleaners of their jobs. Instead, doing so allows them to focus on other areas of cleanliness and allows for a faster turn-around of tables, ensuring a more pleasant dining experience for everyone!

If we are to take pride in our hawker centres, shouldn't we also take ownership in keeping them clean?

This is not only important in the fight against Covid-19, but allows us to further cement our hawker centres as part of our heritage. Wouldn't you rather want to feel proud to take visitors to enjoy Singapore's hawker food when our borders finally open?

Preserving Singapore's hawker culture

But there is hope yet for Singapore's hawker culture. It is slowly evolving, with the younger generation embracing the trade in new and different ways.

Take the young founders of Big Big Fries and an ITE culinary arts graduate who runs his own hawker chain for example. Both have found success in being hawkerpreneurs.

Some youths also stepped up to encourage members of the public to pledge their support during the UNESCO nomination through the Our SG Hawker Culture travelling exhibition in 2018.

Recently, a 26-year-old Singaporean woman suggested that first dates should be at hawker centres as there is minimal stress with deciding what to eat, better quality of food, and it is also wallet-friendly.

While I'm still on the fence over hawker centres as first date venues, the article did take me back to the days when my then-boyfriend-now-husband and I used to meet for lunch at Maxwell Food Centre (our offices were both in the CBD).

There would always be a long queue for the famous Hainanese chicken rice and we would stroll down rows of stalls after our meal to see what delicious food we could try the next time. Good times.

International recognition is a good start. But it takes more than a UNESCO listing to preserve our hawker culture. We don't need an international organisation to tell us what we already know: Hawker culture is Singapore culture. We need to support our hawkers – both the people and the food they make.

So, the next time you are in a dilemma over what to eat, why not head to your nearby hawker centre – and don't forget to clear your tray while you're there!

Do you want to know who I voted for in GE2020?

GE2020 is over and the people have spoken. Results aside, let's focus on what is really important

by Solomon Lim

It is the morning after.

The government has been formed, and with 61.24% of the vote, the PAP has its mandate. With ten seats won by the Workers' Party, the opposition has spoken too. Old strongholds have held and new ones created. Old faces like Lam Pin Min and Ng Chee Meng have left the building. Enter stage left, Jamus Lim and co.

Some of us are rubbing our eyes after the long night of ups and downs. Others are rubbing our hands in glee after the party that we voted for won. Some still are rubbing their faces in disbelief over outcomes expected that turned out different.

But there is one thing that we definitely should not do, that is to rub the noses in it of those who have lost. Cheers have been made, tears have been shed, but there is no room for jeers.

There's more that unites us than divides us.

Over the past two weeks, I've heard Singaporeans praise and protect the party they support, and vilify and insult the other. Tempers have frayed and opinions have been unleashed. I've read well-reasoned arguments and barely coherent diatribes. I've heard tirades over *kopi* at the coffeeshop table and anecdotes over Zoom online.

But despite the differences of opinion, I put to you that we all come from the same place. We all want to have a better Singapore. Where we differ is on how to get there.

250 STORIES OF KINDNESS

The queue to the polling booths snaked through several blocks of flats. *Credit: Solomon Lim.*

Wide-eyed and full of questions

Yesterday, I took my daughter to the polls. She is a precocious 10-year-old who is full of questions.

Five years ago, I carried her in my arms as we voted in Sengkang SMC. It was all a game to her then. A happy holiday where mama and papa queued up with a bunch of other strangers and drew Xs on pieces of paper. Five years hence, she is a little too big to be carried, but she patiently held my hand as we stood in the long snaking line to vote. She still stared wide eyed from the side as I shuffled into the void deck and inked an X on a single slip of paper.

Things may have changed: Sengkang SMC has become a GRC. A PAP ward is now a WP seat.

Her questions are different now. But still innocent. "Why is there such a long queue at the polling booth? (Social distancing, dear, but look, the queue is moving fast, isn't it?); "Why can't I come in with you? (You'll get your chance next time, now you sit over there and wait for me and try not to annoy anyone, k?); and "Can you tell me who you voted for? (I whisper in her ear and she giggles, not so much that she recognises the name, but that she got to share a secret with her daddy).

In five years' time, she will be 15. I wonder what her questions would be then.

She won't get to vote in the next two elections. But despite whatever name I told her, I know who I'm really voting for. For

Celebrating the Singapore spirit 251

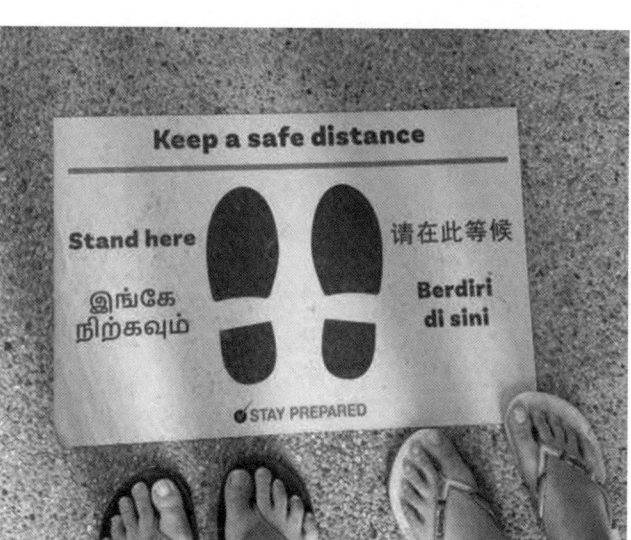

Social distancing reminders stuck on the walkway to the voting booth.
Credit: Solomon Lim.

whom I've always voted for. Not for the ruling party nor the opposition. Yes, of course I made a choice on who to represent me in Parliament. But I'm not voting for them, if you know what I mean.

I'm voting for her.

Our children are the future. It sounds twee and clichéd but that doesn't make it any less true.

Sometimes, our younger generation gets unfairly accused of being blasé towards anything that isn't selfies or bubble tea. But as with all generalisations, it's seldom so clear cut. We may not understand their love for TikTok videos or their need to overshare everything on social media, but different doesn't mean indifferent.

I had a friend tell me how she challenged her son, a teenager not yet old enough to vote, to help her decide who to vote for.

She had been talking to him about the elections and was pleasantly surprised that he had strong opinions of his own. So two days before the polls, she told him: "Tell me who you'd vote for and I'll cast my vote for that person."

She recounted to me later that her son immediately became thoughtful and gave her a well-reasoned argument on who he would vote for if he could.

Does that sound like an apathetic strawberry to you?

And that's the beauty of her choice. It didn't matter who she voted for in the end, because she cast her vote for him.

Don't lose your fervour

Over the past two weeks, I've heard more opinions than I'd have liked. I've laughed at memes as innocent as revived viral videos on pineapples and plans, I've frowned at *ad hominem* attacks, both on the podium and in the online sphere. I've talked a little, and I've listened a lot more.

I had a colleague ask me: "Why are we trying to put out stories on kindness when the only thing people are talking about is the elections?"

No doubt, chances are this week, people would probably be more interested in politics than reading about how a father of a baby born blind got help online or how widows supported each other during the circuit breaker or even how a mum came up with an idea to save millions of disposable gloves each year.

But I feel that there is always room to talk about issues close to our hearts.

To those who have spoken up about such issues, issues on homelessness, on social injustice, on the needs of the vulnerable, on the challenges of foreign workers, on the needs of Singaporean employees, my challenge to you is this: Don't fixate on whether or not the person you voted for got into Parliament.

It is the morning after, the die has been cast and the vote has been made. People have spoken, and the chips fall where they may.

The candidate you supported may have won. Or the party you voted for may have lost. The polls have closed but it doesn't mean your vote has ended.

Don't stop talking about issues that you feel strongly about. Don't wait for another five years before waving your fist in the air. Don't wait at all. Keep talking. Keep acting.

Believe in helping others? There are ground-up movements and volunteer organisations that you can help out at. Believe in speaking up for inequality in society? There are well-intentioned forums where people can discuss these issues.

Talk to your newly-elected MP. He represents you now. He works for you.

Singapore is not perfect. But it is our Singapore. It doesn't matter if we're old or young, single or married; we are all neighbours crammed together on a tiny red dot. Our community keeps us strong. Our beliefs keep us grounded. Our aspirations keep us moving.

Yesterday, I taught my daughter about my duty to my country, a country that she will grow up in, with other children – sons and daughters of Singapore. She doesn't truly understand it. Not yet. And I love that she doesn't have to understand it fully. Not yet.

For now, she has me to decide for her.

After we voted, she ran to a nearby playground and twirled around in that wild abandon that only carefree children have. I watched her as she clambered on a rope and I pushed her (higher, Daddy! Higher!) as she sprawled on a swing.

As I watched her, a quote from the author Roald Dahl came to mind: "Somewhere inside of all of us is the power to change the world."

Today, the morning after, the world has changed for some; for others, it is exactly the same. The birds still sing, the children still play and we have all played a part in taking the next step to keep it that way.

After the dust settles and the confetti clears, we should remember who we really voted for – our children.

About Singapore Kindness Movement

The Singapore Kindness Movement believes that there is kindness in every one of us. We should all aspire to inspire graciousness in each other, one kind act at a time. Spare a thought for the people around us and we can be greater, create a more gracious society, and make life better for everyone.

About The Pride

An online outreach initiative of the Singapore Kindness Movement, The Pride covers current affairs, trending news and provides in-depth commentary on local and global issues that speak to Singaporeans. Focusing on social and community issues, The Pride hopes to inspire people to action – be it through developing personal positivity or taking communal responsibility.